FUZZY LOGIC FOR BEGINNERS

MASAO MUKAIDONO

Meiji University, Japan

World Scientific
Singapore • New Jersey • London • Hong Kong

Published by

World Scientific Publishing Co. Pte. Ltd.

P O Box 128, Farrer Road, Singapore 912805

USA office: Suite 1B, 1060 Main Street, River Edge, NJ 07661

UK office: 57 Shelton Street, Covent Garden, London WC2H 9HE

British Library Cataloguing-in-Publication Data
A catalogue record for this book is available from the British Library.

ISBN 981-02-4534-3

Printed in Singapore.

Contents

List of Figures

List of Tables

Chapter 1

Considering Fuzziness

1.1 Is "Fuzziness" a Vice?

Our common sense tells us making something ambiguous is actually bad. However, in our daily life, we can deal with the ambiguous. We could say it is impossible to live without ambiguity.

For example, let us decide to do something or plan a schedule. Firstly, we choose a direction, make an outline and establish a goal. But, the details remain unknown, or are left to be chosen when we face the problem. It seems impossible to always decide the details of a plan before we carry it out.

On the other hand, ambiguity is excluded in mathematics. Everything is either true or false. Even if you made a very slight mistake the mistake is counted as a mistake on a mathematics examination. Suppose you write 9999, when it should be 10000. A stern teacher might give no points. If you were fortunate, you could gain some consolation points if your teacher were a kind person.

If your examination is marked by a computer, the mistake is, of course, zero point. As an example, consider a mark-sheet style examination, in which you choose an answer from selections and fill in the corresponding box with a pencil. You are not sure if your choice is right, so you fill the box with light black. However, the computer distinguishes your answer and checks if it is marked (black) or not marked (white), and doesn't consider your opinion that this is probably right. In this way, an answer in mathematics is either right or wrong. Moreover, a computer is still only either right or wrong. Thus, a subjective problem such as "mark if you think this great." should not be asked in a mark sense sheet. Also, a machine does not accept

1

the ambiguity which exists in the feelings of a person who marks, although it could be the right mark if you were lucky. However, realities can not always be recognized by yes (1) and no (0), such as in mathematics. As mentioned before, there exists ambiguities everywhere in our daily life. Reality is a sea of ambiguities.

These two "ambiguities", the plan whose detail remains unknown and the mark-sheet marked with light black, seem to be different. Ambiguities are considered to be bad custom in our common sense. Is this true? Although ambiguity may produce a misunderstanding which produces a dispute or is used as something illegal, there must be something which works because of ambiguity. In addition, it is impossible to exclude all ambiguities from our life. This is the time to examine ambiguity and study it from a scientific point of view because of the whole of our life's work with computers which divide everything into black and white and does not allow for the existence of ambiguity.

1.2   Human-Beings Originally Ambiguous

Are our feelings alternatives of yes (1) or no (0)? Although you can calm your nerves by making your feelings clear and definitive, you might feel anxiety because you are concerned if this is really right. When I say either "yes" or "no" I also feel both "yes" and "no" in my mind. We are usually in the that situation.

In another example, we often make an assumption in order to make our communication smooth. Let us suppose that we are debating whether a woman is beautiful or not. It depends on the individuals. Even if the two people estimate that she is beautiful, the result depends on the time, place, view and many conditions. There is hardly ever an absolutely beautiful women as agreed by everybody. On the other hand, there are not so many absolutely unbeautiful women. Most women are in the middle position between them. To begin with, the definition of "beautiful woman" is open to question. The definition of the words "beautiful woman" is clear, and can be found in a dictionary. But, it is impossible to decide who is beautiful because that depends on individuals. Now we know that the meaning of a word is essentially ambiguous. A word is a symbol, which is like a skeleton, and a meaning of the symbol is subjective and extremely ambiguous.

However, we can communicate with each other by exchanging words, that is, by exchanging skeletons. This seems mysterious, too. After all, we believe you can understand that human beings are in an essentially ambiguous existence. In other words, ambiguity is essential and indispensable for human beings.

When we make a decision, our feelings are not stable. We need a lot of mental power when we decide either "yes" or "no." That is because the state of ambiguity is natural. Thus, we are not comfortable when we are asked a subjective question such as "are you very young?" and forced to answer "yes" or "no". Also we feel that a computer and a machine based on mathematics is something dry because mathematics does not allow ambiguity to remain.

1.3   Digital versus Analog

Conventional computers make decisions without ambiguity. Before considering computer logic, let us think about what is meant by digital and analog. The difference is in the way information is represented. Digital is discrete, analog is continuous or approximate. The simplest example is that of a clock. As everyone knows, a digital clock has no hands but only digits and an analog clock has hands.

There is no ambiguity in the case of digital clock because the time is shown by numbers. However, it is clear that numbers change very rapidly and crisply and the numbers shown are an approximation of the proper time. But, if necessary, by increasing the number of digits, it is possible to make it as correct as is required. This is a characteristic of representing information digitally.

On the other hand, let us think about the short hand and long hand of analog clock. Even if units of minute can be read from the minutes hand, the units of seconds can not be read. The accuracy is not very high and there is still ambiguity. However, we can easily get a rough time by looking at it. This is a characteristic of representing information in analog.

As an example, consider making an appointment to meet at 4:00. When it is 3:50, an analog clock tells us how much time to wait till 4 o'clock. However, in the case of digital clock, we first have to remember that one hour is 60 minutes, and then do subtraction, and finally learn there are accurately ten minutes left. Even if you don't need the accuracy you have to go through this process. Somebody told me that it is convenient for memorizing to make an appointment at 11 or 33 minutes after the hour. It is unnatural if he has an analog clock. In this case, it is easier of course to use 15 minutes or 30 minutes. This is because an analog clock represents a meaning by figures directly and a digital clock uses symbols to represent a meaning indirectly. The 11 and 33 minute are used not because the meaning represented by the symbol is easier understand, but because the symbols themselves are easier to memorize.

The conventional computer, a typical example that has no ambiguity, is correctly called a digital computer. This is why it is necessary to understand the difference between digital and analog. That is, information that are treated by a computer is essentially represented digitally. To learn about computers, it it necessary to understand the characteristics of digital representation of information.

1.4 Logic for Computer

As you know, the conventional computer is based on binary logic, in which everything is either yes (1) or no (0) and no intermediate gray. Theoretically digital information is also represented by a combination of 0 and 1. Therefore, digital information can be treated with computers and anything computers can treat is limited to digital representation. That is, the conventional computer works only with input data in which everything is determined as 1 or 0.

This principle where there is no intermediate status is called the law of excluded middle. The binary logic that holds this law of excluded middle has strongly contributed to the miraculous development of computers and the contemporary information oriented society. The advantage of binary logic is to achieve the precision that is required in theory by increasing digits. One more advantage is to be able to program in computers any procedure that is defined clearly and is to be done by computers.

The most important advantage for implementation of machines is to use electronics. The binary truth of true and false can be represented by the correspondence to existence of electrical charge, electric current or voltage. Using electronics makes possible super high speed and small sized computers. Furthermore, since there are only two states necessary, other advantages are that the easier system design, tolerance of a noise, and simpler hardware architecture.

As mentioned, the information oriented society is possible due to computers. Communication and databases help to make society more practical. Digital information representation using electronics makes not only computers, but also digital communication called INS (Information Networks System) and ISDN (Integrated Services Digital Network) possible. Data and knowledge are stored on magnetic disks and floppy disks, and even audio and visual information can be stored as digital information such as on a compact disk. As computers begin to communicate with each other, we can retrieve useful information from databases whenever it is necessary. Thus, we are surrounded by digital information which avoids ambiguity. Although it provides us with a convenient and efficient life, indeed, it seems that we feel somehow unsatisfied and are frustrated.

1.5   Human Beings Forced to Think Suitably for Computer

Because we can discuss and make inference without precise conditions and data, human logic is ambiguous. For instance, somebody tells us to "Slow down when it is raining because rain makes a car skid". However, we don't have to slow down in the case of light rain. We can decide to slow down, of course, in the case of heavy rain.

For another example, we will wait at least an extra five minutes even if our friend promised to come at 5 o'clock. Nobody leaves just because he/she did not come at 5 o'clock. Can we say that "it is raining" when it is light rain? How much speed should we chose when we slow down? How precise is "about 5 o'clock"? There are few people who care about it in detail. We can understand without such a preciseness. We can sufficiently communicate with each other and infer without determining all.

However, it is critical when we use computers to make decisions because a computer can only work if these ambiguous things are written in details without ambiguity and given to the computer with precise definitions of what to do. But, should these issues be defined clearly? Even if it can be done, what does it mean? In the practical view point, though, we have to define them to make a computer work. A computer is not good for doing pattern recognition and abstracting, which are easily done by humans. That is why we are forced to conform to the computer when we use it. From the view of man-machine interface, which is the technology of the interface between human and computer, the victims of the inequality are human beings. This problem can not be solved until a computer can handle ambiguity.

We have seen how ambiguity has been dealt with in science and a technology up to now. Next, let us consider ambiguity again from a historical view point.

1.6 Contemporary Rationalism Due to Descartes

It is said that the binary logic that allows "yes" or "no" is due to Alstoteres, an ancient Greek philosopher. Alstoteres recognized the existence of what should be determined not either "yes" or "no". This means that ambiguity was acknowledged when the study of logic began. But, the main acceptance during the renaissance of symbolic logic, where only "yes" and "no" are assumed, remains up to the present.

There are two kinds of logic. Modal logic is a logic dealing with cases: there is a possibility of true, or there is necessity. This logic also originates with Alstoteres, but it can not be used for contemporary science and technology. Multiple-valued logic is logic where a degree of truth between "yes" and "no" is acknowledged. The multiple-valued logic is being studied frequently these days, but it can not overthrow the established binary logic and remains minor research.

Modern science and technology is definitely based on binary logic that does not allow any ambiguity. Therefore, an exclusion of ambiguity is an absolute and unconditional requirement in modern science and technology. It is agreed that by excluding ambiguity we have established theories and developed applications.

The establishment of modern rationalism has influenced this. Modern science and technology are strongly influenced by Descartes's theory of modern rationalism. His methodology is analytical, in which any complicated problem can be understood by dividing the problem into several smaller problems until each problem can be clearly understood. After every problem becomes clear, they can be combined to grasp the whole problem. The basic idea is that the whole is understood by the composition of each part. Thus the divided parts should be clearly agreed by everybody. An example is the axiom that the sun rises in the east. The combining process also is to be consensus, where objectivity and universality are significant guiding principles. It implies that there is an assumption or a belief that everything has a unique answer which we must discover and clarify.

Is it possible that we can make everything clear? Is there anything that is lost by dividing the problem? If we consider only things that can be clarified by excluding ambiguity in science and technology, we would never handle human subjectivity and feelings that are essentially ambiguous. We would only consider physical issues. Since machines are designed by using theories based on that idea, this consequence applies to machines, too.

1.7 Modern Rationalism at a Deadlock

When Descartes proposed the objective and analytical approach, Pascal claimed the antithesis. He stated that a subjective and synthesis approach are also important, just as Alistoteres claimed the importance of ambiguity when he proposed binary logic. Pascal thought spirit and feelings were central while Descartes thought physics and reason were central. To Descartes's universality, he claimed an individuality. It might be the irony of fate that in order to help his father who worked as a revenue officer, Pascal invented a manual computer which became the original form of today's computers. Descartes could not produce a theory dealing with ambiguity. Pascal became a pioneer in probability, which has been the unique theory dealing with ambiguity up to now.

However, Descartes theories have been favored over time. The spirit of Descartes was succeeded by Ripunitz and Newton, who established modern rationalism. It can be said that the analytical and objective approach has succeeded. Because of Descartes guiding principles and modern rationalism, we have the physically affluent society with fully developing science and technologies. Science makes unknown things clear step by step. The mysterious things are getting trivial. Simultaneously, ambiguity is getting lost. If there is any ambiguity, it means science in that field has not yet sufficiently developed. It can be removed by developing the science. That is a common belief.

It was often unrecognized that quantifying and taking the average of essential human objective characteristics is a disadvantage because in only examining these details there is a missing synthesis viewpoint. Although some sometimes have claimed that science should be human oriented, the antithesis was never major because materialism and modern rationalism succeeded too well.

Nowadays the targets of science and technologies shift from physical issues to energies and information. There is a reason why information was left to now. It is because it is hard to recognize as a target of science since information is so close to our lives. Now we understand the importance of information. Thus, we shall be trying to develop the research field. As information has a deep relationship with our ideology, the research must have an important role in our society. However, it is obvious that the development of information will reach a dead end using a conventional approach because humans are essentially ambiguous, as we have seen before. Therefore, now is the time we have to change the conventional science and technologies approach in which necessary ambiguity has been ignored.

1.8 Information and Ambiguity

What is information? The Japanese word for information is written as "Jyouhou", which means a notification of a mercy. Further consideration shows an interpretation that the mercy is content that we want to communicate, and the notification is like paper or a telephone which can be used to transfer that content. To communicate something, semantics is represented by a medium with some symbols. On the other hand, what we really want to communicate is not the symbols physically sent to the recipient, but the semantics. That is, the information consists of the symbols physically sent and the semantics represented by the symbols. The symbols corresponds to a skeleton that conveys semantics. The semantics, which corresponds to a muscle, depend on interpretations by senders and recipients which are both human.

Up to now, science with regards to information has developed the syntax side of information, and aimed at technologies such as symbols speed, less transport errors, burst transfer, storage and processing. However, information becomes useful only when the human sender or recipient can recognize the semantics. In this sense, it is impossible to ignore the human. This is why information science differ from the others. Hence, we have to face the ambiguity which essentially lies in humans. Of course, this does not cover the case when we just need the syntax of information. Since this does not make sense, we come to the conclusion that research positively assuming the ambiguous would be significant in our highly information-oriented society. While it sounds like this assertion is against conventional modern rationalism that intends to exclude ambiguity, it does not mean that binary logic is useless. It is just insufficient.

We have seen that the tight relationship between humans and computers makes it necessary to establish a theory that positively supposes ambiguity. Thus, any science whose objective is a system consisting of only humans, in other words a society and an organization, would originally involve ambiguity. In fact, however, there have been several attempts to apply technologies of object-oriented science to the social sciences, even though a theory of ambiguity is what is required most by the social sciences.

1.9 Requirement of Ambiguity

Inserting an allowance for the ambiguity looks as if we just gave up on an effort to strictly and precisely examine a target. It also looks like a forged science or false science. Some people claim that essentially ambiguous things such as human feelings or sensitivities must not be studied by science. But, a study ignoring human beings has limitations.

The limitation of the conventional technologies is not the only issue with regards to humans. There are also highly complicated systems and systems which leave subsystems unknown. Is it possible to develop these

systems with conventional technologies? It is a big task to exactly define,
formalize, and model complicated systems. Even if that was completed,
the resulting system could be too complicated to analyze the consistency
of the data. We often need supercomputers. What is really required is
rougher modeling techniques. Even if we could know the general behaviors
of the complicated system, this is impossible. We have two choices using
the conventional strict theories to model the unknown system; just ignore
it, or give proper default values. If, an exact analysis of the system does
not make sense, it might produce meaningless conclusions. The unknown
subsystems should be treated as if they exist. But we have no way to do
this. After all, a theory of ambiguity would be required.

1.10   Aspect of Ambiguity

Up to now, we have used the term ambiguity without an exact definition.
What does it really mean? What ambiguity means is ambiguous. We have
various ambiguities. The following are some semantics of ambiguities:

1. incomplete: not understandable because of the lack of information.
   For example, I can not speak Spanish. So I can't understand something spoken in Spanish. Although the information has a meaning,
   we could not accept it because of lack of knowledge.

2. ambiguity: indefiniteness in several interpretations of one word. A
   Japanese word "hashi" has several meanings; a bridge, an edge, and
   a chopstick . This is called the ambiguity of a word. This property
   holds with not only words but also figures. There is a famous picture
   which can be seen as a face of a young lady and of an old woman at
   the same time.

3. randomness: not yet known since it will be done in future. Which
   side will come up by shaking a dice? Which leg will I use first when I
   leave home tomorrow? These are examples of ambiguity with regards
   to future events. Randomness is often said to be an accident which
   can be calculated with probability.

4. imprecision: not precise or exact. This covers ambiguous cases which
   include errors or "noise". This ambiguity is caused by imprecision of
   information.

5. fuzziness: unable to define, or have a meaningless definition. There
   are the ambiguities with respect to words, that is, ambiguity of semantics. For instance, it is ambiguous as to whether she is beautiful

or not or it is hot or not today. The answers may depend on individual perception.

There are another kinds of ambiguity other than the above. In this book, we consider the fifth ambiguity of fuzziness.

1.11 149 Terminologies Concerning Fuzziness

The word "ambiguity" has a negative meaning. It means often incomplete, sometimes shady. In fact, a Japanese dictionary uses the definition of an ambiguous hotel to mean disreputable hotel. That is why an ambiguous theory sounds like an incomplete theory, or a disreputable theory. Of course, these are misunderstandings. A theory of ambiguity which this book is introducing is a non-ambiguous theory which assumes the existence of ambiguity.

Since the word "ambiguity" has a negative meaning in Japanese, the idea of an ambiguous theory has not been popular. Researchers on the subject have often been misunderstood or slandered. Fortunately, I have hardly ever had such an experience because I have called it "fuzzy theory." This is one reason why the name "fuzzy theory" is becoming more popular than that of "ambiguous theory." We Japanese use the term "fuzzy theory" instead of "ambiguous theory" to avoid misunderstanding, though we are more familiar with "ambiguous." Once I asked a professor what is the best translation of fuzzy theory, he answered "how about a senile theory?" I said I don't like that because it sounds like a senile person. Then he suggested an out of focus theory? It went from bad to worse! So, we had nothing other than "fuzzy theory." This is how it came to be called "fuzzy theory" in Japan. In China, they have a special translation of fuzzy theory because the Chinese word for ambiguity doesn't have a positive meaning either.

Prof. Michio Sugeno, Tokyo Institute of Technology, as one of the researchers of Japanese on fuzzy theory, has surveyed Japanese words relating to ambiguity. There are 149 adjectives to mean ambiguous. Similarly, it is said there are about 170 words in English and about 150 words in Chinese.

What I want to stress here is not the number but the usages. This is a common observation for any languages. There are two usages; prime words such as "ambiguous", "vague", and "dim", and compounds with negative prefix including "un" or "in" such as "inaccurate", "uncertain", "inexact".

1.12   What is Fuzzy Theory?

We have learned that there are various ambiguities. This might be reasonable because indefinite things can vary. While definite things can be determined uniquely, the world of ambiguities is rather wider than that of definite things. Definite issues can be modeled in binary logic. However, it is not safe to compulsorily apply only binary logic to the world of ambiguities. It would be hard to have one unique theory that covers all ambiguities.

The adjective "fuzzy" means boundaries are vague like on a feather. But I don't think fuzzy theory is the only theory for ambiguities. Probability is the only acknowledged theory of the theories, which are studying ambiguities. Both probability and fuzzy theory are theories which can be used to deal with ambiguity. Fuzzy theory can be used for a numerical analysis of ambiguity.

From the above point of view, the whole theories for ambiguities are not clarified yet. What I want to remark on is that probability is abused so often because there is no other theory for ambiguities. It is obvious that the subjective issue "how beautiful" can not be measured by probability. Fuzzy theory is a breakthrough to this drawback. It should be noted that the engineering approach using fuzzy theory to model subjective ambiguity has begun to be successful.

Of course, it is also true that only two theories, probability and fuzzy theory, can not solve all of ambiguities. So, we need yet new theories. Let us conclude that the theory for ambiguities is an unspecified theory including new theories that will be developed in future.

Chapter 2

Before the Invention of Fuzzy Theory

2.1 Invention of Fuzzy Theory — Proposed by Prof. Zadeh in 1965

Fuzzy theory began with a paper on "fuzzy sets", which was published in an academic journal "*Information and Control*," by Prof. L. A. Zadeh, University of California Berkeley, U.S., in 1965, In this paper, Prof. Zadeh named fuzzy sets as those sets whose boundary is not clear, such as "a set of beautiful women," "a set of tall men," and "a set of big numbers." He pointed out that fuzzy sets play an important role in human reasoning for pattern recognition, which is elementary capability, communication of semantics, and especially abstraction. He expanded his assertion into a mathematical theory.

In the conventional set defined in mathematics it must be clear whether any element is "in" or "out," for example a set of men or a set of integers. If it is not clear, it can not be called a set and an object of mathematics. In this sense, the "fuzzy set theory" is a very new proposal.

Why did Prof. Zadeh start to think about such fuzzy sets? He is one of the pioneers and authorities on modern control theory. Modern control theory is very modern, strict and precise. Thus, modeling a complicated system in this theory requires a lot of energy. Although a computer may be used for the processing, we have to specify the details of a process step by step. For example, the control system of robots or rockets becomes complicated. The modeling is extensive and the execution takes a long time. High speed computers can not be useful because of the computation time in the period of the initial stage of computer analysis. Using another example, a computer can be used to predict the direction of a typhoon, but it takes so long that the typhoon will have already passed.

The number of processes to be specified is exponential to the number of elements. Although a computer seems to be almighty, it is inferior to the human brain in certain types of processing. For example, consider a game of chess or go, a popular Japanese game, which we can easily play in our daily lives. However, to examine all possible solutions, even a current super computer would take time as long as the time between the beginning of the earth and now. The targets become still more complicated, even though the computers are slowly getting faster, there would never be time. Clearly, there must soon be deadlock. In this way, he came to the conclusion that the conventional approach, which requires specifying everything in detail, was wrong. Thus, a technology in which the whole system can be roughly defined, that is "fuzzy theory" was proposed.

2.2   Invention of Fuzzy Theory — Limitation of Rigorous Computer Modeling

To tell the truth, there is another important reason why Prof. Zadeh proposed fuzzy theory. Even if the complicated system's problem is solved, the following two issues remain:

1. It is impossible to list all the conditions for a system, because we can not predict what conditions will have an affect on the system. In practical use, the conditions which seem to have influence are chosen and used for control. Hence, the system cannot choose the conditions. In other words, it assumes that the system is controlled only by the chosen conditions. What if an accident happens? We have no way to allow for it. Though we give specific modeling, the system does not avoid an accident.

2. The system parameters, which are conditions assumed to be important for the system, must be determined by some values. However, it is often the case that these values are unable to be fixed accurately. For instance, assume that a system does not work at a certain high temperature, which unfortunately is unknown. The cost for the temperature to be clarified may be large, or man may fail to accurately identify the temperature. We often assume a certain value when we have no information about it, for example 45%. This is frequently done in various areas. A computer requires values to be fixed for its calculations.

Although there are many temporary parameters, the computer reasons based on the conventional strict theories and technologies for analyzing. It manages to produce the results after it repeats its reasoning iterations and spends much time and cost. The results, however, sometimes seem to be wrong. This is reasonable. In most cases, the computation is correct, but the temporarily fixed parameters cause the error. That is, the failure is caused because what is ambiguous is forced to be fixed. Ambiguity should be treated for what it is. This was the big motivation for the development of fuzzy theory.

2.3   Fuzzy Theory Invented by Talking About Beautiful Women — It is Used with Anything that is Dependent on Subjective Reasoning

One of my German friends, a famous researcher on fuzzy theory, told me a secret about fuzzy theory. Here is the real reason why Prof. Zadeh invented fuzzy theory. Oneday, Prof. Zadeh debated with his friend the

issue of which wife was more beautiful. Since this depends on individual perception, the degree of beauty varies. No matter which theory was used to prove it, their opinions would never be in agreement.

There is no theory that can be used to prove a quality like beauty. Therefore, it cannot be determined what "beauty" is. By doing a survey, the percentage of people who think she is beautiful may be just obtained statistically. To fill out the questionnaire, one has to alternatively decide if she is beautiful or not. It is not reasonable to always answer either "yes" or "no." Many want an intermediate answer. Even if statistics show that she is beautiful, would we always agree with them?

This is the story about when Prof. Zadeh thought of the idea of fuzzy theory , which deals with intermediate truth, and indefinite propositions. But, I am not sure this is true story or not, because I have not had an opportunity to ask Prof. Zadeh about its truth.

2.4   Fuzzy Theory Met with Severe Criticism

When Prof. Zadeh published papers on fuzzy sets, researchers showed little interest in his new idea. Most were against it. Some were opposed to his idea because Prof. Zadeh , who had studied strict modern control theory,

changed his opinion from chasing strictness to allowing for ambiguity. Some said he gave up. They claimed that researchers in science and technology must make everything clear and exclude all ambiguities, or try to do so. Thus, Prof. Zadeh was said to be no longer a researcher. The severe criticism was not only about Prof. Zadeh but also about fuzzy theory itself. Criticisms included the following:

- fuzzy theory is not necessary,

- it is not new because it was already proposed by the ancient Greeks.

To publish a paper in an academic journal, the paper is usually judged by some referees. In general, such a controversial paper is hardly ever accepted to be published in a journal. His brilliant achievements in modern control theory might have helped to publish. Furthermore, he was one of the programming committee members of the journal "Information and Control." He told me later that they decided to publish this paper because of his earlier contributions to the journal.

He was disappointed by these negative comment on fuzzy theory. But, not all researchers were opposed to him. The late Prof. Richard Bellman, who is a famous for the establishment of dynamic programming, agreed with the fuzzy theory. His warm encouragement helped Prof. Zadeh to go on studying 'fuzziness.' Later, Prof. Zadeh and Prof. Bellman published a monumental paper together.

Although early on fuzzy theory was mostly ignored, little by little it was studied by more researchers around the world and they were impressed. Research increased in Europe, China, and Japan, using this theory even though the severe criticisms still remained.

2.5 My Personal History — Getting Involved in Fuzzy Theory

Let me talk about why I got involved with fuzzy theory.

I was a graduate student who learned about fail-safe logic at Meiji university. The goal of fail-safe logic is to implement a switching circuit such that a fault might be committed but his would never result in a dangerous state. It accepts the fact that any equipment is subject to being broken. The fail-safe logic is, as it were, safe logic for a failure. Here, we use the word, logic, to mean a logic circuit, which is a component of a computer.

The terminology 'fail-safe' is often used in areas such as airplanes, nuclear reactors, and trains. For example on trains, a signal might show 'to stop' when it should show 'to go', a railroad crossing is closed when it should be open. Though these kinds of errors are troublesome, they are not critical. But, what would happen if it were the opposite? A signal shows 'go' when it should show 'stop'. A closed crossing slips and opens. These errors are serious. The fail-safe logic circuit always behaves so that the latter error can not be made.

First of all, I tried to use binary logic for the fail-safe logic circuit. However, there was trouble. The signal of 'stop' may be interpreted as a stop or a fault. Hence, a system that accepts an action at a signal for stop can violate the fail-safe logic. My conclusion was that for fail-safe logic we need at most three states, yes, no, and unknown or fault, that is, fail-safe logic is ternary logic.

At that time, I read Prof. Zadeh's paper in the Journal of Information and Control, which somebody had recommended to me. I found that fuzzy theory has the same logic as my ternary logic. I immediately wrote some papers, applying fuzzy theory to my idea. Since my professor, Dr. Yasuo Komamiya, who supervised my work in fail-safe logic, is fortunately a long friend of Prof. Zadeh, I wanted to meet him. The chance came to me. Before going to make a presentation at a conference held on the east cost of the U.S. I sent my paper and Prof. Komamiya's letter to Prof. Zadeh. He made a phone call to me from the west cost when I attended the conference. I visited him at the University of California, Berkeley at once. It was in

1977. After he had read my presentation, he said, "Your idea is right. It is what I thought!".

After that visit, in 1979, I stayed with my family in California and worked at the University of California, Berkeley. Although it was too short a period, a half of year, I studied a lot about fuzzy theory as a visiting researcher under Prof. Zadeh.

2.6 On Prof. Zadeh — The Father of Fuzzy Theory

Prof. Zadeh was born in Iran, and graduated from the university of Tehran, Department of Electricity. In the U.S., he received a master degree at MIT and Ph.D. at Colombia University. He worked at Princeton university and then became a professor at The University of California, Berkeley in 1959. As mentioned before, he was a brilliant researcher in control theory and systems theory before he proposed the fuzzy theory.

He is 175 cm tall, slender, and bald. He looks scholarly from the first impression and he is very meticulous. He is known as an expert of mathematics and logic. I personally know that he is very kind, especially to women and Japanese. There are many Japanese researchers who thank him. He knows a lot about Japan, from the cost of Fujitsu stock to the huge electronics market in Akihabara city.

He has visited Japan many times and traveled all over the world. His traveling clothes are unique. He carries things like his passport in a pouch belted at his waist. Though a waist pouch is not so special these days, he was wearing it years ago, which show what a typical American researcher he is.

He is crazy about cameras, so that he always has a camera whenever he travels. Plus, he is skillful with a camera. In his home, there is a portrait of the late president Kennedy which he took. While traveling, he often takes photos and gives them to his friends. Since I have so often seen his kindness, I wonder whether there may be a relationship between kindness and fuzzy theory.

In 1979, he was the only researcher studying fuzzy theory in Berkerly. At that time, most visitors to his house seem to come from foreign countries because his research had been accepted internationally but not in U.S. yet.

He has far fewer American graduate students than international students at school.

He has one informal seminar a week. Researchers join it not only from the U.S., but also from around the world. I, myself, attended it many

times. We used to discuss fuzzy theory from several view points. I was impressed that fuzzy theory was still a developing theory and subject to a various interpretations. I also learned that it is important for us to discuss frankly, which is good for our originality. I still remember that we, Prof. Zadeh and the visitors, were ambitious to promot fuzzy theory which was not acknowledged in the world.

Chapter 3

Fuzzy Theory

3.1 How to Define "Middle Age"

This section defines what fuzzy theory is. I will try to explain it simply without mathematical notations since this article does not aim to give an academic background of fuzzy theory.

Let us take an example of word "middle age". We usually speak these words in our daily life though we don't know the exact years or how long it lasts. So, consider doing survey in order to determine the period. How do you identify "middle age?" Let us have participants answer a particular age using their intuition. It may take a while to answer because a specific age is a bit hard to give. Beside, they may laugh at the image of middle age. Hence, the answer as to what middle age is depends on the individual.

Let assume that we are going to summarize the survey using a computer. We could have a strict definition of middle age, something like the mean, in order to classify a group of survey answers on what age middle age is, according to the result of the survey. Assume that we have the age ranging from 35 to 55 years old. Then, a man who was 34 years old who does not belong in middle age would suddenly become middle aged on the day of his birthday. Similarly, just after the birthday of 56 years old, he would no longer be middle-aged. If time the of the day is also significant, we should take into account the time of his birth. There are few people who remember the time of their birth. Therefore we must give up tying to define a strict model for middle age. We would have to make some assumption. No one wants such preciseness for middle age no matter how exact he is. Obviously, it is not necessary to pursue this preciseness.

We have a vague idea of middle age in our daily conversation. No one

agrees that it begins just after 35 years old. These numerical representations
are conventional assumptions only good for computers. However, as we have
seen conventional theories and computers force us to use the mathematical
model. This means something that is actually continuous and ill-defined
has been forced to be well-defined. In other words, what is actually analog
information has been represented digitally in order to deal with computers.

According to some dictionaries, "elderly" is defined as just 40 years
old. This is far from our impression of it. The United Nation decided that
"old age" is classified as older than or equal to 65 years old. This is just
convenient for statistical manipulation.

Let us goes back to the definition of middle-aged. Figure 3.1 shows an
instance. The horizontal axis shows ages or a period of time, the vertical
axis shows whether 'yes' or 'no'. Yes is 1, no is 0.

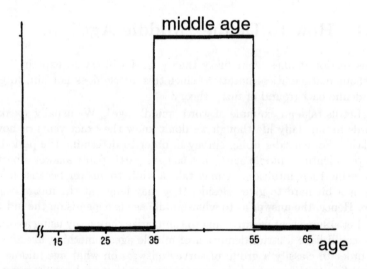

Figure 3.1: Definition of Middle Age in Conventional Sets

One more interpretation is that it is a name of a set, a collection of
objects. For example on ages, the set of "middle-aged" is the numbers 35,
36,..., 55. Any intermediate number in this set belongs to "middle-aged",
all others do not belong. It may be easier if you make 1 to correspond
to belong, 0 to not belong. All standard theories can be explained by
means of set theory. In fact, some researchers are trying to establish new
mathematics by the set theory. Binary logic in which everything is either

'yes' (belong) or 'no' (not belong) is a principle of set theory.

3.2 What is Fuzzy Theory?

What is wrong in the definition of "middle age"? It sounds very unnatural because the boundaries are too sharply fixed. It may make sense if the boundaries were loosely defined. For this sake, we shall consider the degrees of middle age. For example, 35 years old is middle age with a degree of 0.6, and 36 with a degree of 0.65. The degrees may change slightly depending on ages. Figure 3.2 shows how this works. In this definition, there are no extreme steps to middle age where by one becomes old with just one year. You may notice in the Figure that 25 years old is considered middle age by some though the degree is not high. This is an extended interpretation from set theory. Prof. Zadeh calls the new extension of the set theory "fuzzy theory". We have learned that "fuzzy" is an adjective to mean soft, with no definite boundary. In Japanese, we say "Oboro."

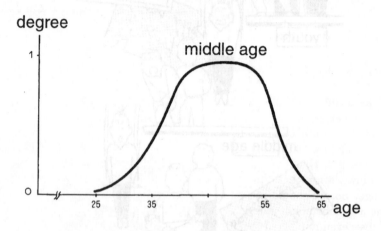

Figure 3.2: Definition of Middle Age in Fuzzy Sets

A fuzzy set is allowed to have an intermediate membership, which is neither 0 or 1 in the conventional set theory. A membership of 1 represents that an element (age) definitely belongs to a set (middle-aged), 0 represents that it does not. A membership of 0.5 shows that it belongs with a half degree.

In a sense, a fuzzy set can include a standard set in a special case. This is the reason that a fuzzy set is generalized from a standard set. Hence, by having membership be restricted within 0 or 1, any theory based on fuzzy theory provides the same result as that derived from conventional theory. On the other hand, fuzzy theory needs to be developed so that it can be consistent with the conventional theories.

Now, we are ready to discuss the semantics and syntax of fuzzy theory. For example, "middle-aged" is a label or name of a fuzzy set by which a behavior of the contents is represented in Figure 3.2. If we consider the example of conversation, words we speak correspond to the label, what it means in the contents corresponds to the figure. In fuzzy theory, the label is said to be a fuzzy set, the figure is a membership function of the fuzzy set. Generally, a fuzzy set is considered to have a label and a membership function together.

In Figure 3.2, the fuzzy set of "middle-aged" is defined over a set of ages, that is, 1, 2, ..., 100. We call the whole set (1,2,...,100) the universe of discourse. The fuzzy set of "middle-aged" is defined over the universe of discourse. Note that the universe of discourse is a standard set on which a fuzzy set is defined.

3.3 Notation of Fuzzy Theory

A fuzzy set has soft boundaries. In contrast, let us call a standard set a crisp set because it has crisp boundaries.

The membership function in Figure 3.2 can be represented by a table. In particular, the table representation is useful when we treat it with computers. For example, consider a dice whose values are 1,2,..., and 6. The set of even numbers can be mathematically defined to be consisting of the three numbers of 2, 4, and 6. Then, let us consider a set of large numbers which has a fuzzy sense. Let's say it is defined by 4, 5, and 6. It sounds somehow strange. So, we should have a fuzzy set represent such intermediate value using a membership function. Table 3.1 shows the answer. Where, column (a) gives even numbers, and column (b) shows large numbers. You can see that number 5 belongs to the fuzzy set of large number with degree of 0.8. We say the membership value is 0.8.

Table 3.1: Membership Function

Dice Number: x	$\mu_A(x)$	$\mu_B(x)$
1	0	0
2	1	0.2
3	0	0.4
4	1	0.6
5	0	0.8
6	1	1

In the table, we distinguish the fuzzy set and the membership function. The label of the fuzzy set is "large numbers", which is assigned to the symbol "B". The membership function of "B" is denoted by $\mu_B(x)$. We write $\mu_B(5) = 0.8$ to mean the number 5 belongs fuzzy set "B" with membership value of 0.8. There is the mathematical way which may be useful for people who are willing to learn fuzzy theory, but the details are omitted here.

Note that the crisp set has a counterpart of a membership function, which is called "characterized function." The characterized function of crisp set A is denoted by λ_A.

3.4   Representation of Subjectivity

So far, we've seen the overview of fuzzy sets. You may have come up with Nowsome big questions: How do we determine a membership value? Why is the membership value 0.6 assigned to 35 year olds for "middle-aged"? Why is the degree of 0.8 assigned to 5 for "large dice number"?

Roughly speaking, a membership value can be decided by whatever you feel, that is, your subjectivity. The value may depend on the individual. You may be wondering how it can be assigned in this way. Now, let me remind you of the classic definition of "middle-aged". It has been given by someone's subjectivity and represented with 1s and 0s. Compared to this classic definition, it is far more expressive when any real number between 0 to 1 is used to define middle ages. With membership values, our fuzzy subjectivity is likely to be represented completely. This is an important point. Fuzzy theory, in other words, provides a means to qualify our subjectivities.

There is a criticism that fuzzy theory has no way to objectively determining membership values. This was the biggest criticism when fuzzy theory was developed. The goal of fuzzy theory, however, is to establish a mathematical theory to deal with subjectivity, given any membership values. Note, that it is not to objectively deal with subjectivity. This is a matter that is argued even now. Fuzzy theory is NOT a fuzzily defined theory. It is a mathematical theory to deal with ambiguities using quantified descriptions in exact methods. I want to stress here, the object is uncertainties, but the method is not uncertain. So, the definition of fuzzy theory is done in a rigorously scientific way.

The conventional theories are based on Descartes's principle whose objects are limited to what can be objectively defined. The uncertain, therefore, is excluded from the list of research topics. Even if it is studied, the representation is forced to be either 0 or 1, even when it seems inconsistent to our feelings. The essence of uncertainties is lost in the methodologies. This is why the result of highly-developed technologies are not comfortable to us.

In fuzzy theory, we take an opposite approach to uncertainties. First, the uncertainties are represented with membership functions, as one feels. Then, the function is manipulated in a method defined in fuzzy theory. If the result does not cover the behavior of the given uncertainties, after the membership functions is tuned we restart from the beginning. We are hardly ever stuck for the values.

The computation involved in fuzzy theory is very simple. Some maximum and minimum are used to get answers. Complicated computation is no longer necessary to deal with uncertainties. Instead, simple and rough procedures are used to have a meaningful result. This is a basic idea of fuzzy theory. It should be noticed that subjectivity becomes possible to be dealt with for the first time since fuzzy theory was developed.

3.5 Operations in Fuzzy Theory

Let us consider one more example of fuzzy sets. Recall the example of the dice, and choose your favorite number of all the numbers on a dice. This is a typical example. Table 3.2 shows a fuzzy set of my favorite numbers. The degrees of membership are given as I like. Next, let us think about disliked numbers. It is the opposite case of favorites. There is a complementary relationship between them. Thus, the fuzzy set of disliked numbers can be determined by the fuzzy set of favorite numbers.

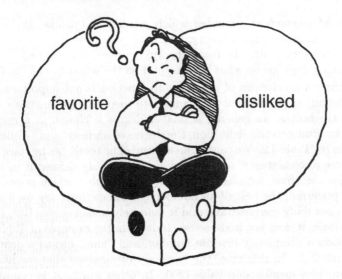

An operation of negation on a fuzzy set is defined by 1 minus the membership function of the set. Although several definitions of negation can be possible, we just say it is defined by 1 minus. That is because simplicity is a virtue in fuzzy theory.

In this way, we have the fuzzy set of disliked numbers as shown in (b) column in Table 3.2. Note that in the extreme cases when a degree is

Table 3.2: Dice Numbers

Dice Number x	C $\mu_C(x)$	D $\mu_D(x)$	E $\mu_E(x)$
1	1	0	0
2	0.3	0.7	0.3
3	0.8	0.2	0.2
4	0	1	0
5	0.6	0.4	0.4
6	0.7	0.3	0.3

(a) C favorite numbers
(b) D dislike numbers
(c) E both favorite and not favorite numbers

given 1 or 0, that is, "one" and "four", a standard "yes" and "no" are in complement relationship, as in binary logic. As we've shown, we should give a new definition of operations so that it can include a conventional theory.

Next, let us consider a number which you like and dislike. It does not make sense in conventional theory, and thus only false (0) is assigned to this contradictory truth. In fuzzy theory, however, this can make sense. The meaning depends on what we interpret as the semantics of "and".

We know a preciseness of membership function is not important, thus simple definition is sufficient to manipulate membership functions. The simpler, the better. In general, a smaller degree is chosen as a result of "and". According to this definition, the degree of likeness "and" dislikeness is given in (c) Table 3.2. We can get an answer! The result can be considered as a degree of consistency, or a degree of how roughly defined it is. After all, we see the "five" satisfies a condition of a number which is preferred and not preferred, the best of all numbers. We sometimes say we like but dislike in our daily conversation, and it definitely makes sense. But, in the world of logic, it does not make sense. Indeed, in the example of Table 3.2, "one" shows a completely favorite number, and "four" means a definitely disliked number. In this case, the fuzzy set of numbers that we like but dislike provides membership value of 0. In other words, it is completely contradictory. While fuzzy set representation provides the intermediate feeling in which we have no contradiction any more.

In fuzzy representation, compared to binary logic, we can feel free to represent our feelings. It must be closer to our real feelings. The law of excluded middle does not hold any more. The law of excluded middle is a principle of binary logic whereby either "yes" or "no" is allowed to be taken. Thus fuzzy logic is necessary where we can take intermediate values.

Conventional set theory and binary logic have three elementary operations: complement set (means negation), intersection (means "and"), union (means "or"). In fuzzy theory, we have defined 1 minus to mean a negation, and taken the smaller to mean "and". Then, how shall we define "or"? Remember that it gives the same answer as binary logic if values are limited to 0 or 1. Moreover, the simpler, the better. Eventually, taking a maximum seems to be the best definition of "or". Prof. Zadeh has adopted this definition.

For example, the fuzzy set of numbers that I like "or" don't like in Table 3.2 has a membership function in Table 3.3 (a). In binary logic, since any truth is either yes or no, such a statement is always true, that is, the degree of membership always is 1, which is called a tautology. In fuzzy logic, as we've seen in Table 3.3, there are meaningful values other than 1.

Table 3.3: Logical Operation with Dice Numbers

Dice Numbers x	F $\mu_F(x)$	G $\mu_G(x)$	H $\mu_H(x)$
1	1	0	0
2	0.7	0.2	0.7
3	0.8	0.4	0.4
4	1	0	1
5	0.6	0.6	0.8
6	0.7	0.7	1

(a) F either favorite or not favorite
(b) G both big and favorite numbers
(c) H both big and not favorite numbers

Let us consider one more example of "and" and "or". Table 3.3 (b) - (c) shows fuzzy sets G and H, which are defined with fuzzy sets in Table 3.1 and 3.2, "big and favorite numbers" and "big but not favorite numbers", respectively. Just taking bigger or smaller is thus simple. The operations of fuzzy sets, "and," "or" and "not," are illustrated in Figure 3.3. Fuzzy set A and B, the intersection "A and B," the union "A or B" and the negation "not A" are indicated.

You may notice some properties such as a negation of the negation of A becomes A itself, and a negation of "A and B" becomes either "A" or "B". These properties hold in fuzzy logic as in binary logic. For example, fuzzy set E in Table 3.2, "favorite and disliked numbers," is identical to the negation of fuzzy set F in Table 3.3, "not favorite or not disliked numbers," that is, 1 minus membership of E is equal to membership of F. This make

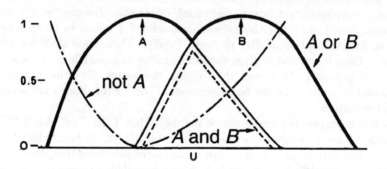

Figure 3.3: Operations A and B, A or B, not A

sense because a negation of what is favorite and non-favorite is equivalent to non-favorite or non-non-favorite (favorite). Let us end the discussion of operations here.

3.6   Concept of Speed and Fuzzy Theory

Alice and Bob take a drive on a highway. Alice says "Please drive the car at a safe speed." Bob answers "Sure," and he drives the car at a safe speed, as far as he know.

Fuzziness is involved in our daily conversations such as in the above context. Fuzziness helps with making communication easier. Let us suppose that Alice expects about 90 km/h to mean "safe speed" and Bob thinks about 70 km/h. With fuzzy theory, this situation can be illustrated in Figure 3.4. If Bob drives in 70 km/h, Alice might request he "Speed up a bit." Both can be comfortable when they drive in the middle speed of their expectations.

Even though their expected speeds are different, since their expected speeds have some fuzziness and there can be an intersection of speeds where both are satisfied. If we use the conventional computer to define "a safe speed" by a strict value with +/- 5 km/h error, Alice and Bob can not reach a consensus.

Our communication can not happen without such fuzziness or a span, where both parties allow for each other. Language always has fuzziness. By representing fuzziness with fuzzy sets, we might be able to make computers that can deal with the semantics of our language. A time to meet with

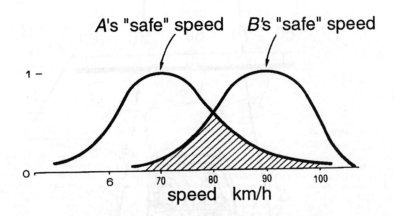

Figure 3.4: Fuzzy Sets "Safe Speed"

someone is fuzzy, and so it should be addressed with fuzzy sets. Suppose we are to meet about five. Then, four is not five but can be said to be about five with lower degree of correctness. Fuzzy sets provide an appropriate description to this example. A relationship between Alice and Bob would rather be given with intermediate degrees than "yes" and "no." The relationship with degrees is represented in fuzzy sets and is called a fuzzy relation.

Let us come closer to the details. Consider a simple example of the relationship between names of diseases and symptoms. Let $a1$ and $a2$ be symbols to mean diseases such as pneumonia or appendicitis. Also, let $b1$ and $b2$ be symbols to show a high fever and a pain. Let suppose that disease $a1$ causes symptoms $b1$ and $b3$, disease $a2$ has symptom $b3$, disease $a3$ has symptoms $b2$ and $b3$, and disease $a4$ has symptoms $b4$.

Table 3.4: Relationship Between Diseases and Symptoms

Diseases \ Symptoms	$b1$	$b2$	$b3$	$b4$
$a1$	1	0	1	0
$a2$	0	0	1	0
$a3$	0	1	1	0
$a4$	0	0	0	1

This relationship between diseases and symptoms can be expressed in

Table 3.4 where 1 means there is something with a symptom, and 0 means there are none. We write R to show the relation. You can see, given a name of a disease, what symptoms might happen. By looking at columns you see possibilities of disease when you have some symptoms. This is how a diagnosis is made. So far, we have assumed a binary logic. In real life, symptoms may be sometimes apparent but sometimes unclear. Hence, we should use an intermediate degree between 1 and 0 as elements of the relation R. Thus, we introduce fuzzy theory here. In this interpretation, values shows possibilities of symptoms that may happen when one suffer from a disease. Table 3.5 gives membership functions. By having an universal set of diseases, $U = \{a1, a2, a3, a4\}$, and a set of symptoms, $V = \{b1, b2, b3, b4\}$, we call the whole Table 3.5 a fuzzy relation over U and V.

In Table 3.5, for disease $a1$, we have a fuzzy set $B1$ over V, in Figure 3.5. This is a fuzzy set of symptoms given disease $a1$. Also, Figure 3.6 gives a fuzzy set $A2$ over U, which shows possible diseases with regards to symptom $b2$. Now we show an interesting technique of fuzzy sets. Using

Table 3.5: Fuzzy Relation R Between Diseases and Symptoms

Diseases \ Symptoms	$b1$	$b2$	$b3$	$b4$
$a1$	1	0.3	0.8	0
$a2$	0.2	0.1	1	0.3
$a3$	0.1	0.8	0.9	0
$a4$	0	0.2	0.3	1

another example, let us suppose that Carol feels bad and is asked some questions (see Figure 3.7). In this example, we assign 0.8 to symptom $b1$, 1 to symptom $b2$, 0.2 to $b3$, and 0 to $b4$. Let B' be a fuzzy set over V to show what symptoms she has. From fuzzy relation R (Table 3.5), we can derive possibilities of her disease by means of a fuzzy set. First, we know symptom b1 has a degree of 0.8, so we take minimum 0.8 and fuzzy set $A1$ (see Table 3.6), which shows possible diseases given symptom $b1$.

Table 3.6: Max-min Calculation

	$a1$	$a2$	$a3$	$a4$
$\min(0.8, A1)$	0.8	0.2	0.1	0
$\min(1, A2)$	0.3	0.1	0.8	0.2
$\min(0.2, A3)$	0.2	0.2	0.2	0.2
$\min(0, A4)$	0	0	0	0
max	0.8	0.2	0.8	0.2

Note that we use a notion of $\min(0.8, A1)$ to mean choosing a smaller value. Simply speaking, this operation has fuzzy set $A1$ truncated at 0.8. It is so simple that you could find out all the rest of the results. Finally, by choosing a maximum from possible values of disease $a1$, we have the resulting value of 0.8. In the same way, possibilities of disease $a2$, $a3$, and $a4$ are given by 0.2, 0.8 and 0.2. Figure 3.8 illustrates the result. Given fuzzy set B' of symptoms (a), using the fuzzy relations shown in Table 3.6, we have a new fuzzy set to mean possibilities of diseases to B'. Conversely, you may notice that a given fuzzy set of diseases for the relation R provides a fuzzy set of symptoms.

As we have seen, if we know the fuzzy relations between U and V, given fuzzy set A' over U, we can compute fuzzy set B' over V, and given fuzzy set B' over V, we can guess fuzzy set A' over U.

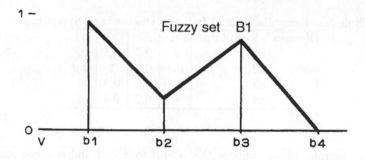

Figure 3.5: Fuzzy Set $B1$ for Disease $a1$

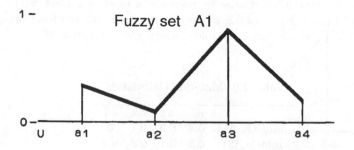

Figure 3.6: Fuzzy Set $A2$ for Disease $b2$

3.7   Consistency of Fuzzy Sets

Two conventional sets have an intersection or no intersection. With fuzzy sets, there are degrees of intersection. Thereby we introduce a consistency (or consensus) of some fuzzy sets. Recall the fuzzy set of middle age in Figure 3.2. The membership value of 30 years old is 0.6, and thus we say the consistency of 30 years old and middle age is 0.6. In the example, we considered consistency of fuzzy sets and an element of ages, which is a crisp value. Next, we extended the definition to consistency among fuzzy sets.

In Figure 3.3, we have two fuzzy sets, A and B. We may consider semantics such as middle age or old age. The first thing we have to do to define a consistency of A and B is to compute the intersection of A and B, which is indicated by the dashed line in Figure 3.3. We define the consistency of A and B by the highest membership value at the intersection.

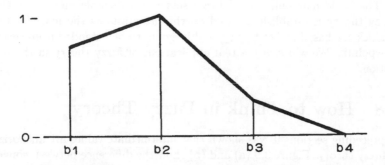

Figure 3.7: Fuzzy Set "Symptom" B'

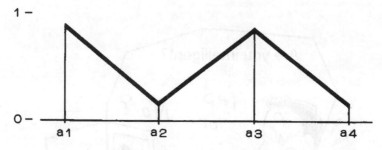

Figure 3.8: Fuzzy Set "Disease" for B'

In the example in Figure 3.3, we have 0.75. This is one of the frequently used techniques called a max-min operation, since we pick the maximum value out of values defined by the minimum. Thus, a consistency of fuzzy sets is computed by max-min operation.

In a previous example, we computed the fuzzy set of big and favorite dice numbers, in (b) Table 3.3. This is an intersection of two fuzzy sets "big numbers" and "favorite numbers," and thus we have the consistency of them by picking the highest value, 0.7, at the dice number 6. Similarly, in example of Figure 3.4, the consistency of Alice's and Bob's safe speeds is at about 80 km/h, say 0.7.

The concept of consistency of fuzzy sets is one of the key ideas in fuzzy theory. Even if either/both of two sets are crisp, the max-min operation still works since 1 and 0 of crisp value are included in a special case of fuzzy sets. But in such case you can use simplified computation rather than maximum and minimum.

The basic manipulation of fuzzy sets is thus simple and reasonable. Fuzzy theory is established based on the fuzzy sets as the mathematical theories are based on set theory, and in going to be extended from several viewpoints. We will study a real applications of fuzzy theory in the next section.

3.8   How to Think in Fuzzy Theory

In preceding sections it was shown that intermediate values are authorized in fuzzy theory. Figure 3.9 (a) and (b) show the difference between conventional theory (a) and fuzzy theory (b). For example, consider if you were asked "Are you an intelligent person?" Give your answer. In the figure,

the horizontal axis gives answers ranging 0, meaning "no," to 1, meaning "yes." Figure 3.9 (a) shows a case when you answer "yes." You have only two choice, 1 or 0. If you are allowed to answer with fuzzy sets, you may feel free give your opinion and an example of 0.8 is indicated in figure (b).

Wait. Are you okay if your intelligence is given by just 0.8? It might be less than 0.9 but must be more than 0.6. Figure (c) shows this case, where you can have greater expression This expression is called an interval

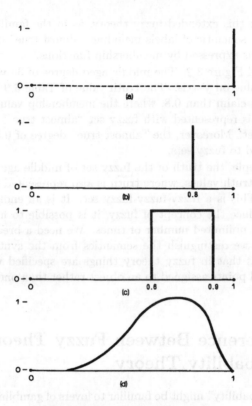

Figure 3.9: Degrees of Truth

truth value. However, it looks like the crisp definition of middle age. It just replaces x-axis of ages with truth values of 0 to 1 and it sounds unfamiliar that the truth sharply changes from 0 to 1 at the 0.6. Okay, let's recall the idea of fuzzy theory and extend it further, that is, making things fuzzier. In this way, we got figure (d). Note that figure (d) comes from figure (b) or (c) by making crisp definition fuzzy, as Figure 3.2 is the fuzzy version of the set of ages in Figure 3.1.

This can be a more expressive way to represent the semantics of the words "almost true" than the way of numerical values. Figure (d) defines the membership function of "almost true." In the context, we could say (a) and (b) are special fuzzy sets meaning "absolutely true" and "definitely 0.8."

In fuzzy theory, there is an extension that deals with truth values expressed by words instead of numerical notations. It is called a linguistic truth value. In this extended fuzzy theory, as in the familiar example of middle age, the semantic of labels including "almost true" depends on the individual and is expressed by membership functions.

Let us recall Figure 3.2. The middle-aged degree of 38 years old is 0.8, which is the value on y-axis. The truth value of Table 3.9 (d) provides a more uncertain claim than 0.8, where the membership values of fuzzy set "middle-aged" is represented with fuzzy set "almost true." This is called a fuzzy-fuzzy set. Moreover, the "almost true" degree of 0.5 is 0.8, which can be extended to fuzzy sets.

In the example, the truth of the fuzzy set of middle age is represented with linguistic truth values, where truth is also represented with linguistic truth values. This is a fuzzy-fuzzy-fuzzy set. It is an endless procedure. Once we introduce the concept of fuzzy, it is possible to have fuzzy representations an unlimited number of times. We need a break point. This point is where we distinguish the semantics from the syntax. What we should notice is that in fuzzy theory things are specified with some dynamic weighted points assigned to an object rather than one stable unique point.

3.9   Difference Between Fuzzy Theory and Probability Theory

The word "probability" might be familiar to lovers of gambling. Probability theory comes from gambling. For example, a probability of even in rolling dice is 0.5, a probability of one in one roll is 1/6, that is, 0.1666666.... The probability of 1 means it always happens, and the probability of 0 means it never happen. (In theory, it may happen with probability of 0 if there are infinity large samples.)

When fuzzy theory was proposed, there was a criticism that it was equivalent to probability theory. It could be replaced by probability and, therefore, fuzzy theory was useless. The range of probability is the same as fuzzy theory, that is, a decimal from 0 to 1. However, we should notice the uncertainty fuzzy theory deals is essentially different than the one that probability treats.

First, let us consider the uncertainty treated in probability. There are six sides to a dice. Even before we rolls a dice, we completely know there are six possibilities from 1 to 6. The probabilities of each side landing up are equally likely and 1/6. The uncertainty comes from the fact that we can not see which sides is up before we roll a dice. We can not predict the future, hence there is uncertainty. After rolling, we can know everything.

This is an uncertainty called randomness. In probability theory, the total probabilities of all possible events must sum up to 1. This is a condition of probability. As we have seen, probability used to be the only theory which could deal with some uncertainties until fuzzy theory was developed.

In statistics it is too hard to assign probabilities to all possible events because of the strict condition that the sum of all probabilities must be 1. While it is very useful that probabilities provid exact numbers, large amounts of computation are needed. Still, probability is very efficient and used for many applications. However, if we don't know at all the possibility of event, or have not enough information about the likeness of event, any complicated computation is meaningless.

The uncertainty of fuzzy theory is basically different than randomness. For example, think about meeting a very beautiful woman tomorrow. We cannot know whether we will be alive until tomorrow. This is an issue of probability. Now, let's say, you actually meet a women the next day. Can you decide if the women is beautiful or not? This is the issue of fuzzy theory. The object of fuzzy theory is a subjective uncertainty that you can not determine even after the event actually happens.

Probability is based on set theory. Fuzzy theory is based on fuzzy set theory. Since the (crisp) set of labels of fuzzy sets is a crisp set, we can consider the probabilities of them. This means both theories can work together.

3.10 What is Possibility Theory

We have learned that a membership value of a fuzzy set expresses the degree to which an element belongs to a fuzzy set. This is one interpretation of membership values. We give a number of interpretations to membership function including a certainty factor to the attribute represented by a fuzzy set, a degree of truth, a degree of satisfaction, and a degree of possibility. Professor Zadeh expands fuzzy theory to the possibility theory, where membership values are interpreted as possibilities of events.

In the context of Figure 3.4, Alice and Bob were satisfied with a speed of about 80 km/h and the membership value was 0.7, which was considered a degree of satisfaction. Now, we can consider the degree of possibility that both are satisfied. It is likely that in our daily life, a point from 0 to 1 means the possibility rather than the probability. No one cares about the condition of probability when 0.8 can just mean some possibility. There is no way to determine whether the condition really holds or not. Therefore, the probability can do nothing for the subjectively given numbers.

3.11   Quantifying Uncertainty

To end this section let us go back the issue of uncertainty in language. The essential uncertainty of human beings might come from the language we have used to communicate in because the semantics are uncertain. Information that we want to express is continuous and analog. But, we can communicate with each other with the digital symbols of language. The semantics of the transferred symbol are reconstructed in each mind. For human and computer interaction computers need to understand the semantics of our language. Computers receive a language, and then look up the semantics of the words. The syntax and the semantics correspond to a fuzzy set and a membership function.

Fuzzy theory provides a method for computers to quantify the semantics of the language. The uncertainty of the language caused by subjectivity is represented by a membership function which gives arbitrary precision to expressions. The computer can have knowledge only if it stores the quantified semantics of language as its internal memory. The fuzzy theory aims to provide an effective tool for humans and computers.

Chapter 4

Applications of Fuzzy Theory

4.1 Uncertainty not Accepted in Inference Based on Binary Logic

Fuzzy theory has been applied to various fields. The aim of this section is to introduce the underlying principles rather than talking about a particular application. The early applications were mainly in the engineering fields, including fuzzy control. These days, the applications are slightly extended to social sciences, including medical diagnosis or a stock investment system. Let us begin with a fuzzy inference which gives an underlying theory for most fuzzy applications.

The inference characterized in logic and implemented on computers is a bit different than we have thought. First of all, let us have a simple overview of inference in logic. The inference consists of statements - A implies B, B implies C, than A implies C -. This is called a syllogism. Basically, when a premise that "A implies B" holds, we know that B is true if A is true, and conversely, if B is false then A is false.

Let us take an example that "a rich man is stingy". In logical expression, it says "if a man is rich then he is stingy". Whether it really is true or false, we assume it is true. Let's say, my friend Alice is rich. From the premise, the conclusion is that she is stingy. On the other hand, if Bob is not stingy, then he is not rich. However, even if Carol is stingy, we don't know whether she is rich or not. The converse is not always true. This is what we can learn about inference in school.

That scheme of inference was formalized and abstracted from the observations of behavior of our daily inferences. Note that all these are based on the principle of binary logic - the world of yes and no. For example, let us study the following the process when we come to the conclusion that he isn't rich from a premise that he isn't stingy. If we presume Bob is rich then he must be stingy. But we know he is not stingy, so the assumption that he is rich contradicts the premise. Since he is either rich or not and we know he is not stingy, therefore, he must be not rich. Notice that the binary logic principle of "excluded middle" plays an important role in the above inference.

In the above inference we used instances such as rich and stingy without the semantics of the words. These can be replaced with symbols A and B. Thus the logic is called symbolic logic.

Symbolic logic is used in making inference in computers. Since the computers work according to the binary logic, the symbolic logic matches the computers very well. Besides, symbolic logic is also used in designing the computer itself.

4.2 Daily Inference

By the way, do you believe the proposition that "a rich man is stingy"? Is it wrong? It might be hard if we always accept the principle that everything must be either true or false because almost all propositions are uncertain. If Bob is little bit rich what follows from the fact?

The conventional computer has no semantics and thus assigns an independent symbol to the fact that he is little rich, say C. The proposition C is neither A nor not A. The C has nothing to do with A. The computers can reach no conclusion from the premise that A implies B and the fact C, though C sounds something like A.

As we've seen, inference based on binary logic is obviously an effective tool but is quite different than the inferences that we make in our daily life. Inferences based on binary logic have only yes and no. Furthermore, they have no semantics.

Let's go to an another example – a beautiful women has a short lives. It can be taken implicitly, as beauty and long life seldom go together, or explicitly as a beautiful women dies earlier than normal. This is what we often guess in our daily life. Note that the all the facts, including the rich, the stingy, the beautiful, and the short life, are hard to determine by either true or false. These are fuzzy terms. Inference rules, such as rich implies stingy, are also fuzzy. We can easily handle these fuzzy rules and facts, while computers can not. This is a fundamental weak point of machines, although our lives are surrounded by these fuzzy concepts.

4.3 Fuzzy Inference

Professor Zadeh uses this similar example as fuzzy inference: "If a tomato is red then it is ripe," and "This tomato is very red," implies "This tomato is very ripe." This is an example of inference that we usually do. It is hard to do on conventional binary-based computers because the premise is a fuzzy rule and the words "red" and "ripe" are fuzzy facts which convey uncertain semantics.

Professor Zadeh developed a new inference method for computers which uses fuzzy sets to specify these words, and has membership function to convey the semantics that the words mean. This is what we call a fuzzy inference. Let's take a look at the formalization made by Prof. Zadeh, which might looks like mathematics. Recall the example that if a woman is beautiful then she has a short life. We write this using fuzzy sets,

"if X is F then Y is G".

Here is an explanation of this notations. The X is a variable that means someone who belongs to a particular set of women. Let U be a universal set of all women we discuss. For example, U = "Alice, Barbara, Carol." The variable X is one of them. Next, the F has a membership function that assign a degree of beauty for each members of U. You know, F is a fuzzy set over U. You can give Alice any degree of beauty, $mu_F(Alice)$, by your subjectivity. The membership function is providing semantics of the fuzzy set to mean beautiful women.

The variable Y shows an age when she dies. The Y is presumably from 1 to 100 as all possible ages humans usually die. We use V to denote the universal set of Y, that is, $\{0, 1, 2, \ldots, 100\}$.

We have a fuzzy set G over V to mean a short life. The membership function of G, $mu_G(y)$, shows the degree of short life given age y in Y. Of corse, you can give membership values as you think.

Now, let us consider a given fact:

"She is pretty,"

which can be written as

"X is F'".

Where X is a variable on U, and F' there is a new fuzzy set over U to mean "pretty". Note that the fuzzy set F' does not necessarily have to be equal to the fuzzy set F of the premises. This is one of characteristic of fuzzy sets. We have already seen that binary-based symbolic logic can derive no conclusions from incomplete premises.

4.4   Formalization of Fuzzy Inference

Using fuzzy sets, the fuzzy inference can be formalized by,

"If X is F, then Y is G," and "X is F',"

where F and F' are fuzzy sets over U.

Given F = "beautiful", F' = "pretty," and G = "short life," what we can say about the span of life of pretty women? We wish to have a consequence that

"Y is G'"

from the premise. The G' is a fuzzy set of the set of ages, V. There has been proposed several ways to compute G', though we don't yet have consensus as to which is the best.

The method proposed by Prof. Zadeh is to identify from F and G a fuzzy relation, R over U and V, which has a consequence over G' on V' from the given F'. This is the same method we used when we guessed diseases from given symptoms. The other inference methods use the same inference scheme but the definitions of R are different. There is no unique manipulation in defining fuzzy relations. This means that there are many types of fuzziness for which a right fuzzy inference is defined.

Whatever fuzzy relation is defined, we expect that the conclusion, G' would be closer to "short life" as the fuzzy set "pretty" more closely matches "beautiful". If the two fuzzy sets were independent, then we would know nothing about her life span, which means there would be an unknown conclusion.

The consequence G' is given by a membership function other than language. If we want to have human readable outputs, we need to find the optimal words to approximate the membership function. This requirement leads us to an interesting problem of linguistic approximation of fuzzy sets.

Now, let us turn to the problem: what if a premise such as "a beautiful woman has a short life" is not completely true. Let's say, it is "almost true," that is,

"If X is F, then Y is G" is almost true.

The "true" of "almost true" can be assigned to a linguistic truth value defined with a fuzzy set, T, on the set of truth values from 0 to 1. The result can be seen as follows.

First, in the same way as the previous example, we compute the fuzzy relation R over U and V from F and G. Next, for the fuzzy set T to mean "almost true" we modify the fuzzy relation R, call it R'. The procedure to compute R' given R and T is also known, but will not be examined here. Finally, with the obtained R', we have the fuzzy set G' of V from the R' and the fact F'. While it seems to be little complicated, we can have the fuzzy consequence for any premise. In the process, the fuzzy set and membership functions play an important role. Uncertain knowledge is described in our spoken language, which gives a label specifying a fuzzy set. Then, the knowledge is translated into membership functions, which provide semantics to our knowledge. The membership functions are appropriate representations in computers and are retranslated into language before they show the output to us. In this way, the inferences involved in our daily life can be implemented in computers. This all is because of the fuzzy sets.

You may be curious about the usefulness of fuzzy inference because we took the silly example that beautiful women have short lives. Let us consider an example, "slow down if it rains," which can be applied to slow slightly down when it showers, and also to slow down a lot when there is a rainstorm. This is an advantage of fuzzy theory.

It has been impossible to do this when we use only conventional symbolic logic. This is one of the expected advantages of the field of fuzzy theory. We'll see this later when we look at the fuzzy expert system and fuzzy control, which come from fuzzy inference. Fuzzy inference provides us with a method to use our daily word-based inferences on the computer for the first time.

4.5 Artificial Intelligence and Uncertainty

Artificial Intelligence, AI for short, has been an active research topic recently. Although AI sounds like an attempt to make an artificial brain, it actually is different than expected.

It has been impossible so far to create an artificial brain that is able to think like humans, and it is not likely to happen in the near future. Then, what does artificial intelligence mean? Our appropriate definition is applying computers to fields where human beings are able to do well. In other words, it aims to provide an intelligent human-computer interface so that computers can assist us in involved intelligent activities.

Let us go back to the history of AI. Computers were used to do numerical computations, and then used in processing information. Along with changes in its objectives, the name "calculator" is changed to "information processing equipment." Now, they can deal with knowledge information and are called artificial intelligence systems. Computers now use highly-developed technologies. They have broadened the application areas close to our social lives without being noticed by most of us. Furthermore, in conjunction with communication and database technologies, computers have become a big part of our information-oriented society. Dependency on computers is going to be even higher in the future.

When computers got involved in a part of our intelligent activity, people expected to have computers think and infer something as we do. The research on artificial intelligence is motived by this expectation. You may wonder what the term "intelligent" means? Please notice that addition and multiplication used to be thought of as "intelligent" jobs. Nowadays nobody would accept this definition. Calculations are no longer part of our modern definition of "intelligent."

There are two approaches in research on artificial intelligence. One is to clarify the mechanisms of our brains and implement an artificial brain from the physiological point of view. It sounds like an approach toward true artificial intelligence, though almost all mechanisms are still unknown. The other is to employ conventional computers in the jobs that human can handle better than computers. Current research is mainly on the latter. The research on artificial intelligence is on the frontiers of computer science, and thus the content varies as time goes by.

However, while the latter approach is where most research is currently being conducted, the former approach is one of the most important and interesting science themes and is going to be required to be done actively in the future before computers can really think like humans. Whether the latter approach can be true artificial intelligence or not, applied computer techniques are particularly significant since the computer has been developed enough to deal with knowledge information. We believe that practical intelligent systems will be invented and applied widely in engineering and industrial fields.

4.6   How to Make Computers Thinks

How in principle can intelligent work be made by the current computers ? It is well known that the computers around us are called the Von Neumann machine. They are digital computers. The Von Neumann machine is a computer that stores a set of commands into its storage equipment as a program, which is then executed step by step.

The question as to what class of works can be implemented in the Von Neumann machine had already been answered by the great mathematician, Alan Turing, even before an actual computer was developed. He mathematically clarified what is possible with the Turing machine, a mathematical model of computers. It is known that what the contemporary computer can do is limited by what the Turing machine can do. This fact means that the limitations of computers are already clear. The computer can only deal with what it knows how to deal with. This is a general statement with regards to any machine.

You may think, "why don't we have computers learn how to do it?" But, you have to at least specify how to learn. This means computers can learn in only the way specified. But, the way we learn, which is the biggest function of human brain, is not yet clarified. This is the main theme of the other artificial intelligence approach.

We don't believe in the hypothesis that the way of learning is uniquely given when one is born. It is free from any a priori knowledge. It is hard to believe that we were born into the world with only one way of generating creativity/inspiration/intuition. The truth may be made clear as the research on our brain is improved. This is an essential point in how humans differ from machines. So far nobody can answer this question though.

The human brain is not based on the Von Neumann machine. Since analog information is conveyed through our nerves, it is not digital processing. From this observation, we see that the mechanism of contemporary computers is different from that of human beings. This makes sense because the digital computer is not perfect.

Professor Yasuo Komamiya, a pioneer in the development of computers, said that it is important for us to find a restriction that makes computers usable and does not disturb human activity. I agree with his claim. Research on artificial intelligence can not achieve the aim of developing a computer that can think as humans do without dealing with the "uncertainty" with which we are surrounded. Furthermore, to develop computers as our assistants to problem solving, uncertainty will link humans and computers with a flexible communication.

4.7 Expert System — The Frontier of Artificial Intelligence

The expert system is an example of a large and practical success of artificial intelligence. The expert system is a computer system that makes a decision as a human expert can do in a very limited area with the knowledge that a specialist has, e.g., a diagnosis of a system or an evaluation of the stock market. What is the knowledge of an expert? How can it be represented in a machine readable way? Let us begin with these questions.

First of all, we survey the expert. Next, his know-how in the area are written in a set of rules called If-Then style rules such that "IF something happens THEN do something." Based on symbolic logic, computers executes an inference process and outputs a optimal decision as human experts do.

The difficulties in the process are in acquiring the knowledge from the experts, and in converting these to If-then rules. Because the expert does not recognize explicitly the knowledge as a rule, it is hard to define the exact rule. The knowledge is expressed as much as possible in sentences such as "do something in one case, otherwise do something else." To deal with the incomplete sentences in the framework of symbolic logic, they should be represented by a form that is either true or false. This is hardly possible.

The actual expert system was developed with few regards to this difficulty. Thus rules are likely to be long and in complicated forms. Such systems sometime fail, or need to be fixed somehow and tuned many times. The drawback comes from the issue in the science technologies that binary logic is used to analyze uncertain or complicated objectives.

The goal of the expert system is to employ human knowledge and experience in the field where conventional technologies do not apply. The processing of uncertainty is, therefore, a crucial step to the expert system. From this observation, we see that the expert system needs fuzzy theory and fuzzy theory needs the expert system for its most important applications. Furthermore, since the If-then style rules are used in usual expert systems, fuzzy inference is absolutely appropriate for the framework of the expert system.

4.8   Fuzzy Expert Systems

In this section, we study the expert system, using fuzzy theory. First, ask human experts. Have them write their know-how in a natural language, i.e., the sentences in which they usually speak. Convert the language into a bunch rules such that "if ... then it becomes ..." or "if ... then do ...." By setting the words in the rules as fuzzy sets, the experts give subjectively the corresponding membership functions to the words. Invoke the fuzzy inference we've already discussed. If the result is not as expected then fix the membership functions.

Given a set of inputs and outputs, there are some algorithms to identify an optimal membership function. The rules used in the fuzzy expert system consists of some fuzzy sets, and so called fuzzy rules. The attempt to have computers make inference using uncertain human knowledge in conjunction with fuzzy sets opens up a new field. We will discuss fuzzy control in a later section, showing a typical application of the fuzzy expert system.

4.9 Using the Fuzzy Expert System to Drive a Car

Let study a simple example of the fuzzy expert system. In Figure 4.1, one is steering the car. For simplicity, we consider only the direction of the car. Seeing the direction, we control the angle of the steering wheel. It's even easy for children.

Let us try to generate a fuzzy rule. We know that "if the car is veering right, turn the wheel to the left," "if the car is veering left, turn the wheel to the right," and "if the car is driving straight, keep the wheel as it is." Letting x denote an angle of the car, and y the angle of the steering wheel, we have the fuzzy rule as following:

Fuzzy rule 1: If x is right, then y is turned to the left,
Fuzzy rule 2: If x is left, then y is turned to the right,
Fuzzy rule 3: If x is straight, then y is kept the same.

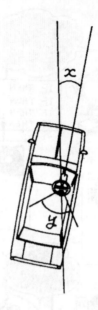

Figure 4.1: Steering the Car

We have six fuzzy sets, that is, the angles of the car, left, right, straight, and the movements of the steering wheel, turning to the left, the right, and keep the same. Now, we give the fuzzy sets with the membership function defined in Figure 4.2 (a),(b),(c), and Figure 4.3 (a), (b), (c), respectively.

Next, we are going to identify fuzzy rule 1. We have the universal set of angles of the car, U, ranging from -15 degree to $+15$ degree. The universal set of angles of the steering wheel, V, consisting of -45 degree to $+45$ degree. We apply the simplest method to determine a fuzzy relation between U and V, though there could be several proposals for determining this. For simplicity, the set U consists of $\{-15$ degree, -10 degree, -5 degree, 0 degree, 5 degree, 10 degree, 15 degree$\}$, the set V consists of $\{-45$ degree, -30 degree, -15 degree, 0 degree, 15 degree, 30 degree, 45 degree$\}$. Other degrees can be linearly interpolated between two points which are closest to each other.

Under this assumption, we have fuzzy rule 1 represented by the fuzzy relation $R1$, as shown in Table 4.1 (a). According to the simplest method, called the truncating method, when the direction of the car is definitely veering to right, i.e., the membership value "the right" of 10 degree in

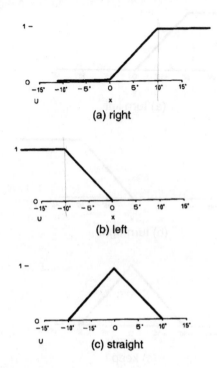

Figure 4.2: Membership Function "Angle of the Car"

Figure 4.2 (a) is 1, give the entire fuzzy set "turning to the left" on V. However, when the membership value is small, say 0.5 with regards to 5 degree in Figure 4.2 (a), truncate fuzzy sets of "turn left" with the value of 0.5. In the same way, we give the fuzzy relations $R2$ and $R3$ in Table 4.1 (b) and (c) as the fuzzy rule 2 and 3, respectively.

Let's say the angle of the car is veering +5 degree. Fuzzy relation $R1$ outputs a membership function A in Figure 4.4, and fuzzy relation $R2$ gives membership function B. But, $R3$ gives nothing. The result of fuzzy inference in the fuzzy expert system is defined by the union set of all fuzzy sets generated by each fuzzy rule. The rules are examined independently one at a time. This is different than the conventional expert systems. In fuzzy expert system, an inference is done roughly and superficially.

You may think the membership function used in this example is too simple to be used in a practical system. No. The actual membership

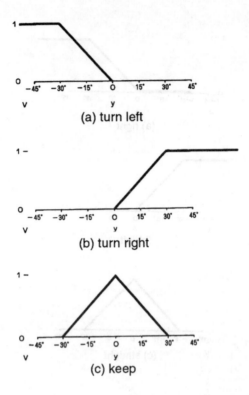

Figure 4.3: Membership Function "Movement of the Steering Wheel"

functions used in real systems are as simple as in this example.

We are going to give a verbal interpretation of the resulting fuzzy rules. When the car is veering slightly to the right (5 degree), apply both the rule that gives the steering wheel to the left and the rule that keeps the wheel at the same angle, which results in the middle angle between the "left" and the "same." In order to actually drive a car, we have to decide on a certain angle for the steering wheel. Thus, instead of the resulting fuzzy set, we should somehow extract a single crisp value from the fuzzy set. This process is called "defuzzyfying," and there are many proposals for it. In this example, we compute the mean of points that give the highest membership value in the fuzzy set. In Figure 4.4, we see −45 to +15 degrees have membership value of 0.5, thus we have the mean of −15 degree, which has us steering to the left slightly. Figure 4.5 illustrates the results for each of the angles of the car +10, +7.5, +5, +2.5, 0, −2.5, −5, −7.5, −10 degrees.

Table 4.1: Fuzzy Relations $R1, R2, R3$

(a) Fuzzy Relation $R1$ for Representing Fuzzy Rule 1

		V						
		-45	-30	-15	0	+15	+30	+45
	15	1	1	0.5	0	0	0	0
	10	1	1	0.5	0	0	0	0
	5	0.5	0.5	0.5	0	0	0	0
U	0	0	0	0	0	0	0	0
	-5	0	0	0	0	0	0	0
	-10	0	0	0	0	0	0	0
	-15	0	0	0	0	0	0	0

angle of car

(b) Fuzzy Relation $R2$ for Representing Fuzzy Rule 2

		V						
		-45	-30	-15	0	+15	+30	+45
	15	0	0	0	0	0	0	0
	10	0	0	0	0	0	0	0
	5	0	0	0	0	0	0	0
U	0	0	0	0	0	0	0	0
	-5	0	0	0	0	0.5	0.5	0.5
	-10	0	0	0	0	0.5	1	1
	-15	0	0	0	0	0.5	1	1

angle of car

angle of steering wheel (Power)

You can make sure it makes sense.

The examples we have seen concern cases where an input is given by a crisp value. What will happen if we give fuzzy input? The fuzzy inference easily covers the case. Given fuzzy input that "the car is veering slightly right," which is represented by a fuzzy set in Figure 4.6 (a), we have the output as shown in (b). Try to examine the results.

These simple rules make it possible to drive a car. The point is that the way to make a decision is similar to what we do. In the fuzzy rules, there is no consideration for the exact values of weight and speed of the car, which are required by the conventional control method. Since driving a car is possible in this simple way, you may be suspect that the conventional control theory could provide better control than fuzzy rules do. This is partially true. However, the success of the fuzzy expert system shows us the fact that simple fuzzy rules are able to deal with a complicated system just as human beings can deal with something that is never done by exact methods.

(c) Fuzzy Relation $R3$ for Representing Fuzzy Rule 3

		V						
		-45	-30	-15	0	+15	+30	+45
U	15	0	0	0	0	0	0	0
	10	0	0	0	0	0	0	0
	5	0	0	0.5	0.5	0.5	0	0
	0	0	0	0.5	1	0.5	0	0
	-5	0	0	0.5	0.5	0.5	0	0
	-10	0	0	0	0	0	0	0
	-15	0	0	0	0	0	0	0

Figure 4.4: Output with $x = 5$

Although fuzzy control still has some issues to resolve, including automatic tuning of fuzzy rules and fuzzy sets and the design of systems involving trial and error, there have been a number of successful applications in practical systems.

4.10 The First Successful Example — Fuzzy Control

In the beginning of fuzzy theory, when Professor Zadeh presented fuzzy set theory in 1965, the research interests concentrated only on theoretical themes. It was a time when fundamental research was establishing fuzzy theory. Researchers were mainly interested in what happened if underlying set theory of mathematics was replaced by fuzzy sets. All mathematical theories that were based on the crisp binary set theory would be new theory if fuzzy sets were applied to them.

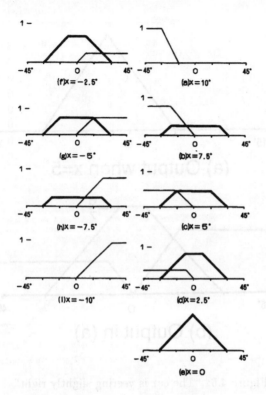

Figure 4.5: Outputs with Various Angles x

For example, applying fuzzy sets to standard integers such as 2 or 3 we have fuzzy numbers such as "about 2" or "almost 3". The fuzzy numbers follow fuzzy arithmetic. Similarly, the integral was extended to a fuzzy integral. Topology, a subject in mathematics, hatched a new mathematics called fuzzy topology. There was criticism that fuzzy theory was a game of mathematicians without any application. However, fuzzy inference, which comes from binary logic based inference as we've seen in the above section, was formulated and made a breakthrough in the application of fuzzy theory to engineering. Fuzzy inference, proposed by Professor Zadeh, was used in automatic controls of a steam engine by Dr. E. H. Mamdani, London University, in 1974. Fuzzy control had its birth with this application.

In the later 1970s, there was a lot of research on fuzzy control. In 1980, the first practical system, which was a fuzzy controller for a cement plant, was used by a Danish corporation. In 1980s, many practical systems

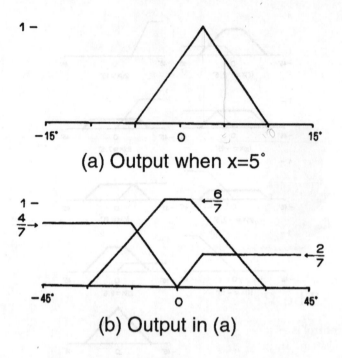

(a) Output when x=5°

(b) Output in (a)

Figure 4.6: "The car is veering slightly right"

began to be used in several fields. In Japan, Tokyo Institute of Technology and Fuji Denki Corporation developed a practical fuzzy control system in a water purifier system. With their successes, fuzzy control attracted the attention of industry. Additionally, there were many successful applications reported in newspapers including an automatic cruise control for subways and a control system in elevators.

Fuzzy control is especially useful in areas where given factors are subjective, e.g., how comfortable is a ride, or where human operators can work better than machines. Nowadays, Japanese fuzzy control technology is the highest level in the world. Also, Japan is leading the world in applications of this technology to industry. In the U.S., it has been reported that fuzzy controls is being used by the military.

4.11 The Principle of Fuzzy Control

Fuzzy control is an application of fuzzy inference. It is exactly like the fuzzy expert system. In fuzzy inference, rules are described in natural language using fuzzy sets, and converted to fuzzy relations. One difference between fuzzy inference and fuzzy control is its output. Fuzzy inference takes fuzzy or crisp input and generates a fuzzy set, whereas the output of fuzzy control needs to be a single value rather than fuzzy sets. This is because the output is then fed to machines as an actual control signal. Moreover, the input to fuzzy control is usually given by a numerical value that may come from sensors in the system. Usually fuzzy control has multiple inputs. We have seen that fuzzy inference can be implemented by a fuzzy relation. In fuzzy control, we would rather have visualized representation of fuzzy rules because it makes simple the truncated method with multiple inputs. Let's see the details.

Fuzzy rules are used to control the target in fuzzy control. For example, let us suppose the following fuzzy rule:

"If the temperature, x, is high (A_i) and the difference of the temperature, y, is small (B_i) then close a valve, z, slightly (C_i)"

where A_i, B_i and C_i are fuzzy sets. The fuzzy rules used in fuzzy control are sometimes called fuzzy control rules.

In Figure 4.7, we denote n rules by $i = 1, \ldots, n$. The above fuzzy control rule is i-th rule.

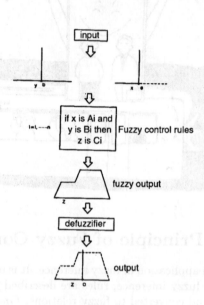

Figure 4.7: Overview of Fuzzy Control

Let us say we have input: $x = a$ and $y = b$ and fuzzy rules A_i, B_i, and C_i as illustrated in Figure 4.8. First, compare the given inputs with the conditional part of the i-th rule and obtain the degree of i-th consistency. We have the minimum values of A_i's consistency, which is membership value A_i of a, and B_i's consistency, that is, membership value B_i of b. The reason why we adopt the minimum comes from the interpretation that the rule states the case when both conditions high (A_i) AND small (B_i) must be satisfied. With the A_i's and B_i's consistencies a_0 and b_0, we show the total consistency, c_0, as shown by $c_0 = \min(a_0, b_0)$ in Figure 4.8. The i-th output is the fuzzy set C_i in the latter part of the rule whose membership values are limited up to the c_0.

Computing for each of the n rules, we have n outputs. Which outputs should be chosen as the answer? Even if we pick the largest fuzzy set as the

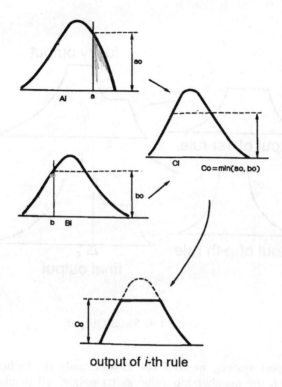

output of *i*-th rule

Figure 4.8: Example

answer, two fuzzy sets are not always comparable since fuzzy sets can not be put in numerical order because one fuzzy set might contain a smaller fuzzy set. Alternatively, we determine the output by the union of the all fuzzy sets whose membership function has the highest value for each n value. We illustrate how it works in Figure 4.9. In the figure, the result of the union is the fuzzy set labeled by fuzzy output.

You may notice that we did the same thing when we studied the car driving example, in which we just used fuzzy relations represented in a table. The illustrated method in this section makes it be easier to understand the truncated algorithm. This way can be easily extended to an example that has more complicated rules of logic. The truncated algorithm is not a unique method for fuzzy inference but is frequently used in most applications.

Finally, we extract one value from the union fuzzy set. In the example

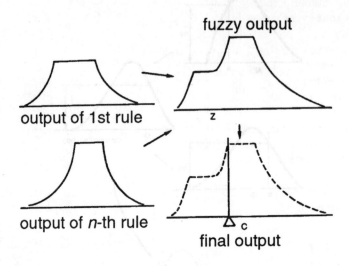

Figure 4.9: Final Output

of fuzzy expert system, we took the mean of only the highest points. In general, with the membership value as its weight, all points are used to compute the mean value. This way is called a center of gravity method and a general operation that gets a crisp value from fuzzy sets is called defuzzifying, that means the inverse of fuzzifying.

4.12   Design Characteristics of Fuzzy Control

We have seen how fuzzy control works. You may have a feeling that it is the way everybody thinks. This is because fuzzy control is closer to our thinking than conventional control theory. The fuzzy control rules and membership functions can be provided by human experts. Alternatively, the designer of the system gives tentative values and then fixes them through experiments. In this section, we consider the characteristics of fuzzy control.

The largest difference from conventional control technology is fuzzy rules consisting of <u>If-then</u> style rules, which are given by human experts. This is the first point. The second point is fuzzy sets which can approximate uncertainties of human knowledge. That comes from the subjective knowledge of the human expert. The third point of the characteristics of fuzzy control is that every rule is independently and simultaneously examined in fuzzy control.

In the conventional system using a non-If-then style rule base, whenever the exact condition that matches the rule to the given input, i.e., $x = a$ and $y = b$, is found, the conclusion part of the chosen rule is added to the rule base as a new rule. Then, the system holds on inference in multiple rounds.

Let us consider the conventional system from the view point of these conditions of rules. Letting U and V be a universal set, the conditions specified by these rules partition the set of U and V into several definitive subsets.

For instance, we show five areas, $M_1, \ldots, M_5$, distinguished by five conditions of rules in Figure 4.10. Let's suppose an input $c_0 = (a, b)$ is given.

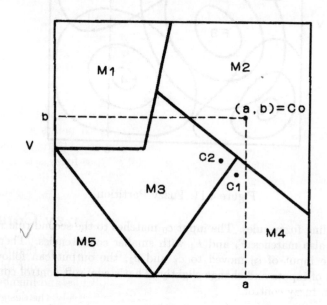

Figure 4.10: Crisp Partition

The input only matches the second rule and does not satisfy any other rules. In this case, the result would be identical to a conclusion specified by the second rule. Every time the input is changed from c_0 to c_1 and then c_2, the result could have remarkable changes depending on applied rules M_4

and M_3.

Meanwhile, fuzzy control roughly divides the set of conditions U and V which have some dependencies since conditions are defined by fuzzy sets. As shown in the Figure 4.11, all five of rules are examined for the given input of c_0 in one round and we have five different fuzzy sets as the result of inference. In the figure, F_1 to F_5 are fuzzy sets descried by five

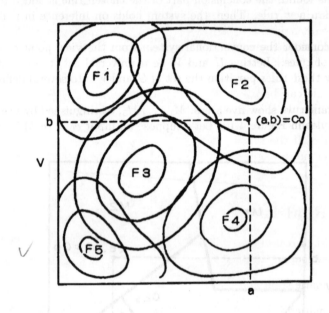

Figure 4.11: Fuzzy Partition

corresponding fuzzy rules. The input c_0 matches to the second rule F_2 the most and also matches F_3 and F_4 with smaller consistencies. Therefore, even if the input of c_0 moved to c_1 and c_2, the output can follow the movement of inputs and change slightly. That's why soft control could be achieved in fuzzy control.

4.13   Fault Tolerance Characteristic of Fuzzy Control

In general, a complicated process involves uncertainties in its rules. Nevertheless, conventional inferences are involved in multiple rounds with rules which are forced to be either "yes" or "no." Because of this, the results could be meaningless. In this difficulty, fuzzy control makes inferences in a single round, using fuzzy sets that can fully represent the uncertainties, and comes to rough conclusions as human beings do.

Let me point out one more important characteristic of fuzzy control. It is a robustness against fault. For example, suppose that the second rule in Figure 4.11 was broken and did not work at all because of human error in design or hardware malfunction. Although the output was wrong, rule 3 and rule 4 can compensate for the loss of the second.

We could see this effect in the example of fuzzy expert system in Figure 4.6. In (b), the left fuzzy set comes from fuzzy rule 1, the middle comes from rule 3, and the right comes from rule 2. You can see that error in one fuzzy rule can be covered by the remaining two fuzzy rules. This is because every rule somehow contributes to the output. Meanwhile, conventional systems are subject to the influence of the fault. In Figure 4.10, given input c_0 if the second rule, which decided the output without any help of other rules, was broken, the system would have no output and thus lose control.

4.14 Real Example of Fuzzy Control

Here is a list of real applications of fuzzy control which have been written about in newspapers and journals:

1. Automatic train and subway control

2. Automatic load controller of containers

3. A control system for automatic elevators

4. A filtration plant system

5. Robot arm control

6. Temperature control in a blast furnace for glasses

7. A control system of an incinerator

8. Cooling process control

9. Incinerating process control

10. Controller of welding robot

11. Temperature control in boiling water service

12. Automatic car speed controller

Some examples may be unfamiliar to outsiders. The first example of the automatic train control is famous. The system, developed by Hitachi, Ltd., is for the automatic running of a subway in Sendai city using fuzzy control. The fuzzy control rules concerning degree of safety, comfortableness for passengers, energy costs, time costs, and a preciseness in stopping points were acquired from motormen's experience and actually used to control an unmanned subway. Compared with conventional control techniques, the system reduces the number of times breaks are applied, which helps reduce energy cost and makes the run comfortable for passengers. When the second International Fuzzy System Association Congress was held in Tokyo in 1987, there was an optional tour to ride on the subway in Sendai. It has a good reputation.

We have already learned from the history of fuzzy theory that professor Zadeh gave up pursuing the accumulation of exact theorems to control very complicated large system and decided to present fuzzy theory as an antithesis to conventional control theory. Recently, he said that he did not expect fuzzy theory to be used in the application of controls. Fuzzy theory moved from its origins motivated by the issue of control theory. As you know, there have been many developments of fuzzy control in Japan. Fuzzy theory was invented in the U.S. by Iranian professor Zadeh. The application of controls originated in Europe. Now, the fuzzy control industry is growing in Japan.

4.15 Application in Social Science — Academic Uncertainty

Question: Which have uncertain criteria, engineering and science or social science and the humanities? Of course, the latter have. The reason is because the target in social science and the humanities is human-beings. No one can live without uncertainties. The target of engineering is objects.

However, human factors are sometimes required in engineering because the developed system is eventually used by humans. This is especially so when the target's dynamics are too complicated, the research target has too many unknown factors, the system is required to be harmonized with humans, or the system is expected to behave like humans, under these circumstances uncertainty is necessary information that needs to be addressed.

This shows that engineering requirements has had a strong influence on the development of fuzzy theory. Compared with humans, machines are very definite targets. However, it has been proven that even though the target is obvious, the rough identification and indistinct inference in fuzzy control sometimes can handle the target better than the rigorous method. This sometimes make possible what has never been done before. These facts show the effectiveness of fuzzy theory.

But, what really should be applied to fuzzy theory may be the social sciences rather than engineering. The theory just happens to have been developed for practical use in engineering. The original effectiveness could be made clear in the social sciences and humanities, since the target is humans for which uncertainty is inevitable.

There is one difficulty: the number of uncertainties considered in the social science can not be compared with those in engineering. Thus, the fuzzy theory just provides a means for these uncertainties, though it can not cover all of them.

So far, some difficult theories that were developed in natural science or engineering have been applied to the humanities. I doubt that the attempts using these methods were always successful. Presumably, it is almost impossible to apply theories that are supposed to be used for distinct objects to definitely uncertain objects.

In engineering, probability has been used to deal with uncertainty. In social science, mainly probabilities and statistics based on probability are used even now. Every uncertainty is assumed to be random and is dealt with in the framework of probability and statistics.

We don't agree that subject matter such as personal preference should be discussed with probability. In this sense, fuzzy theory is expected to have an impact on the social sciences and the humanities. Unfortunately, fuzzy theory is not known to many researchers in that field. There are no remarkable results yet. But, some researchers in engineering are trying to apply fuzzy theory to non-engineering fields, and some researchers in social sciences are beginning to use it as a new measure. We will consider some possible application in the social sciences and then see the trend of fuzzy applications.

4.16   Evaluation of the Risk of Smoking

We have already seen how fuzzy control works. The goal is to control the object so that its behavior will be as desired. The technique is based on fuzzy inference. The idea of fuzzy inference is applied to a fuzzy expert system, which can not only be used in engineering. The application for objects becomes fuzzy control. Thus, applying fuzzy inference to the stock market, we can have the fuzzy expert system for stock investments. In fact, a real system was developed and used by a stock company. Clearly, the fuzzy expert system is usable for many issues in the social sciences. We will show some examples based on consistencies of fuzzy sets, which is less complicated than fuzzy inference. Let us consider the following example of smoking.

A doctor does not think that smoking less than 10 cigarettes a day is harmful for health (safe). He presumes that more than 50 smokes definitely is absolutely harmful (dangerous), and from 20 to 30 smokes is potentially harmful (suspicious). His understanding about smoking can be illustrated with fuzzy sets in Figure 4.12. The horizontal axis shows the number of smokes a day, and the membership function expressing the risk of smoking is indicated on the vertical axis.

Alice's satisfaction of smoking is given by a fuzzy set, A ,on the figure, that is, she is satisfied if she has about 10 or 20 smokes a day. The doctor's diagnosis is given by the points of agreement of each of the fuzzy sets, safe, caution, and danger.

We know the points of agreements are given by the highest value at the intersection of two fuzzy sets. In this case, Alice has the safety degree of 0.9, the degree being caution of 0.9, and the danger degree of 0. Also, we have Bob's fuzzy set, which means he requires about 40 or 50 smokes a day. The case shows the danger degree is 0.85 and his safety degree is almost 0.

The membership function used to give the diagnosis can be provided by the statistics or by the doctor's subjectivity. This example shows a way to give a subjective diagnosis, which might be too simple for real use. If the patent is required to be classified, we can take the label whose value is the highest. You might also have noticed that in the example, the horizontal axis gives continuous numbers.

4.17 Fuzzy Survey

When you fill out a questionnaire, you may notice that there are some uncertain choices other than "yes" nor "no," for example, "I don't know," "neither", "partially agree," "probably." This is what fuzzy theory can be applied to. Similarly, the idea of fuzzy theory has already been applied to several fields unconsciously. For example, the computer dating system, which finds your favorite type of partner, must have a database of fuzzy information. As fuzzy theory is developed, these independent techniques will be able to be unified and considered in a uniform framework.

Let us see one more example about questionnaires. In the previous example, continuous numbers are indicated on the horizontal axis. This example has discrete factors about personal preferences to independent questions. Two students in my laboratory volunteered to answer the following questionnaire. When the statement is right, the answer is 1, otherwise the

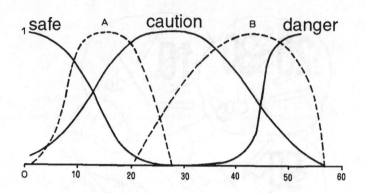

Figure 4.12: Fuzzy Sets with Regards to Smoking

answer is 0. But, if it is neither right or wrong, the intermediate number is answered with its degree. The following are the statements

C1. The PC is my friend.

C2. I always wait until the last minute to do something.

C3. I am never frugal with money for my favorite dishes.

C4. I like mathematics.

C5. I prefer regular coffee.

C6. I never sacrifice pleasure for study

C7. I am polite.

C8. I always meet my obligations to attend ceremonies.

C9. I hate a job which requires human communication.

These nine statements are not likely to be answered either "yes" or "no." The original questions come from a subscriber's survey of the magazine, "Nikkei Electronics."

Mr. I and Mr. S answered as in Table 4.2 (a). We will estimate the degree of their consensus on the survey. To get the degree of consensus, we

use the max-min operation, in which the maximum value is taken as the output among nine minimum values between I and S for each question. In this example, question $C3$ and $C6$ have the same maximum value of 0.6. This means that there is a consensus on "being frugal with money for dishes" and "denying the sacrifice of pleasure for study." The degree of their satisfaction is 0.6. Now we survey the third and fourth students, A and B, and show the results in Table 4.2 (b).

It seems to me that I is a typical urban oriented person and S is a person who prefers the country side. Let us call I's type the urban, and S's type the country. Then, we can estimate A and B's degrees with regards to the urban type and the country type. We find out that A has the urban degree of 0.6 and the country degree of 0.7, and B has the urban degree of 0.9 and the country degree of 0.8. In the social sciences, this kind of classification is many useful for more in-depth analysis.

Although the estimation is too simple, this shows a way that fuzzy data (the answers to the questionnaire) can be classified roughly in fuzzy theory.

Table 4.2: Subjective Survey

	C1	C2	C3	C4	C5	C6	C7	C8	C9
(a) I	0.9	0.9	0.6	0.8	0.4	0.6	0.2	0.1	0.1
S	0.2	0.1	0.8	0.1	0.7	0.9	0.6	0.7	0.9
(b) A	0.6	0.2	0.7	0.1	0.5	0.5	0.8	0.7	1.0
B	0.9	0.9	1.0	0.6	0.8	0.1	0.4	0.3	0.1

4.18   Fuzzy Similarity

We can adopt other measures for fuzzy data such as questionnaires. For example, 0.8 and 0.6 have the same difference of 0.2 to 0.4 and 0.2. Both pairs can be considered as the same degree of agreement. In this interpretation, the exact same values have a perfect agreement and 0 and 1 have the biggest degree of difference. In this sense, we define the new measure for agreement as 1 minus the difference between them.

We are going to have the measure of I's agreement relation among the restricted questions within $C1, C4, C5$ and $C8$. The result is shown by the matrix in Table 4.3. It shows the fuzzy relation between a set of $C1$, $C4$,

Table 4.3: Fuzzy Relation

	$C1$	$C4$	$C5$	$C8$
$C1$	1.0	0.9	0.5	0.2
$C2$	0.9	1.0	0.6	0.3
$C3$	0.5	0.6	1.0	0.7
$C4$	0.2	0.3	0.7	1.0

$C5$, $C8$ and itself. Note that the matrix is symmetric since in the definition, the difference between C_i and C_j is equal to that of C_j and C_i. For the same reason, all diagonal values are 1 in the matrix. These properties are called symmetric and reflective. The matrix is illustrated visually in Figure 4.13. We sometimes call this a fuzzy graph.

Using another example, we will consider if the friend of a friend is a friend? In real life, this relation does not hold. Indeed, I have two friends who are not friendly with each other. But, for simplicity, we assume that any friend of a friend is a friend. This assumption is a property called transitivity.

In Figure 4.13, we have the degree of agreement of 0.9 between $C1$ and $C4$, and 0.6 between $C4$ and $C5$. Then, what degree shall be assign to between $C1$ and $C5$ by way of $C4$? According to the principle of simplicity in fuzzy theory, we choose the minimum value in 0.9 and 0.4 for the assigned

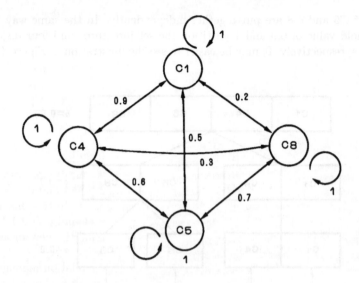

Figure 4.13: Fuzzy Graph

degree. However, something strange would happen in Table 4.3. The direct agreement degree between $C1$ and $C5$, which is given as 0.5, is less than 0.6 that of the indirect agreement via $C4$. Between $C1$ and $C5$, there are a total of five routes: $C1 - C5$, $C1 - C8 - C5$, $C1 - C4 - C5$ and $C1 - C8 - C4 - C5$, and $C1 - C4 - C8 - C5$. To define the consistent degree, we take the maximum value for all routes. This is also a max-min operation. Finally we have the new fuzzy relation which satisfies the transitivity as shown in Table 4.4.

Table 4.4: Similarity Relation

	$C1$	$C4$	$C5$	$C8$
$C1$	1.0	0.9	0.6	0.6
$C2$	0.9	1.0	0.6	0.6
$C3$	0.6	0.6	1.0	0.7
$C4$	0.6	0.6	0.7	1.0

We say it is a similarity relation if the relation is symmetric, reflective and transitive as shown in the example. A similarity relation has an interesting property. For example in Table 4.4, if we collect elements which have values greater than 0.6, then all elements are collected into a single set. If we choose elements greater than 0.7, a pair of $C1$ and $C4$ and a pair of $C5$ and $C8$ are put together independently. In the same way, the threshold value of 0.9 and 1 partition the set into three and four disjoint subsets, respectively. It may be easier to see the illustration in Figure 4.14.

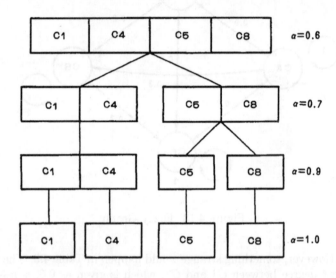

Figure 4.14: Fuzzy Graph

In this picture a parameter, alpha, indicates the strength of association. The partitioned subsets correspond to the modified fuzzy graph in which any branches less than alpha are eliminated in Figure 4.13. Observation of Figure 4.14 shows that if the threshold is 0.7, it has the relationship among questions as follows: his feeling that he likes PCs is close to that of that he likes mathematics, and the preference for regular coffee is as important to him as the obligation for ceremony is. While the two likes have nothing to do with each other, the value of this information is only to show how important these things are to the subject. what this shows is that fuzzy theory can be used for classification of questions in a survey, and is also good for estimation of relationship among classes.

4.19   Difficulty with Conventional Data Bases

A database is a set of data that can be processed by computers. The goal of a database system is to provide useful data concerning given keywords

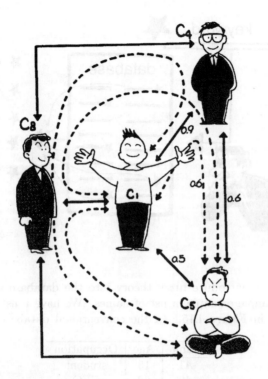

from the data stored in the system. There are broad scales of databases, from a personal address book that runs on PC to the huge storage of articles managed by newspaper services. Another example is a well-known technical reports database system operated by The National Center for Science Information Systems. Anybody can access such large databases over the Internet. The database is an important technology in establishing the public infrastructure for our information oriented society.

In most database systems we can only find the articles and references that are exactly matched with the given keyword. Some systems have a relevance table among keywords, which is used to give some related keywords to the original keywords and shows boarder articles than others. Though, this is not common. The conventional database is based on binary logic, where the result of matching is forced to be either a success or failure. There is no degree of meaning. The relevance table can be considered as a method to convey the semantics. Nevertheless, a search for an uncertain request is not accepted in the conventional database.

What if we introduce fuzzy theory into the database systems? Lets consider a simple example, a list of names. We have a list of names and occupations in Figure 4.15. In the conventional database it is possible

Name	Age	Occupation
A1	15	student
A2	60	CEO
A3	20	salesman
A4	28	engineer
A5	30	lecture

Figure 4.15: Basic Data

to retrieve the age and the occupation from a name, and also to retrieve the list of names given an age and an occupation. Then, can we look up a "young and intelligent person" in the system? The keywords, "young " and "intelligent," can not be used because these words are not in the database. Furthermore, the words "young" and "intelligent" depend on individual opinion, that is, these words are appropriate information for fuzzy set representation.

Figure 4.16 shows an example of the structure of a fuzzy database. In the figure, the fundamental data corresponds to the table in Figure 4.15. The additional database linked to the central management system is used for an interpretation of fuzzy requests.

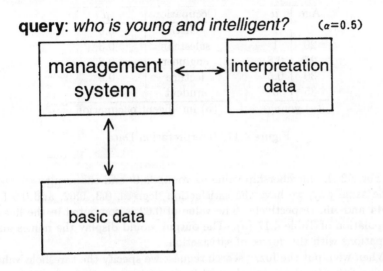

Figure 4.16: Fuzzy Database

4.20 Fuzzy Database

When the search request for a "young person and an intellectual occupation
" is given, the central management system identifies that the keywords,
"young" and "intellectual occupation," are fuzzy sets over the set of ages
and of occupations. In actual syntax, we write something like "age=young,
occupation=intellectual" to specify the request. Next, the system retrieves
the semantics of the keywords from the interpretation database. In this
example, we have the interpretation data in Table 4.17. The data, such
as ages, has a continuous membership function, which is represented with
some sample points as shown in (a). In general, the intermediate value
between points can be linearly interpolated.

For each person in the fundamental database, we are going to estimate
the degree of satisfaction to the request of "young" and "intellectual occupation". Person $A1$ (Figure 4.15) is 15 years old, and according to the
definition of membership function in Table 4.17 (a), he has membership
value of 1 to set "young." But, since he is a student, his membership value
to the set "intellectual occupation" is 0.5. The condition means that both
"young" and "intellectual occupation" must be satisfied, that is, the minimum value shall be taken. Finally, $A1$ has the degree of satisfaction of

Age	μ		Occupation	μ
0	1		CEO	0.6
20	1		salesman	0.3
25	0.8		engineer	0.8
30	0.5		lecture	0.9
35	0		student	0.5
(a) young			(b) intelligent occupation	

Figure 4.17: Interpretation Data

0.5. For $A2$ the membership value to young is 0, and the result is 0, too. In the same way, we have the satisfaction degrees, 0.3, 0.62, and 0.5 for $A3, A4$ and $A5$, respectively. The value of 0.62 is computed in the linear interpolation of Table 4.17 (a). The output would display the names and occupations with the degree of satisfaction.

When we input the fuzzy search request we specify the threshold value of alpha, for example, to tell the system to retrieve entries having a degree greater than 0.5. In this case, we would get the result of the ordered list in Figure 4.18 and would know A4 has the most reliable satisfaction degree of 0.62.

```
A4   28   engineer   0.62
A5   30   lecture    0.5
A1   15   studnet    0.5
```

Figure 4.18: Sample Answer to Query

The remaining problem is how to define the interpretation database. Of course, the user is allowed to assign any value to the data that he likes. Default data can be overwritten by users. For the case when the required word is not registered in the interpretation database, good systems should be ready to add any new fuzzy sets.

It can be said that the fuzzy database is a system extended by the interpretation data which specifies personal preference so that the interpretation can be customized. Hence, by just replacing the interpretation database with a new one, the system can handle any uncertain request.

In the example, we used a crisp fundamental database, which could be extended to a fuzzy database so that instead of specifying an exact value such as "30 years old," fuzzy labels such as "young" could be stored. In this extension, the degree of satisfaction is computed by the agreement of two fuzzy sets. A fuzzy database with features specifying fuzzy labels has actually been developed.

4.21 Real Applications

We have shown some simple ideas which it is possible to apply to the social sciences and the humanities. The real applications are not as simple as we have seen. Sometimes, an understanding of mathematics is required.

The applications of fuzzy theory to economics, the social science, management, and psychology have been published so far. In these application there are some common approaches: decision making in uncertain environments, fuzzy modeling, and uncertain structure identification. Decision making is a topic in operations and research (OR). Many methods have been proposed based on crisp set theory, including linear programming and dynamic programming.

There are also probability based methods including regression, time sequential models, and quantitative theory. These methods have already been extended to fuzzy linear programming, fuzzy dynamic programming, fuzzy regression, fuzzy sequential models, and fuzzy quantitative theory.

For instance, fuzzy linear programming was developed early. In conventional linear programming, given the restriction, say the limit of $1,000, the optimal solution is required. The restriction is illustrated in Figure 4.19 (a). Even if the true optimal solution was at $1,100, the conventional linear programming method could not reach the solution. Whereas, a general constraint in our daily life is not so strictly defined. A restriction of less than $1,000 is often equivalent to about $1,000. The basic idea of fuzzy linear programming is to put on fuzzy sets as the constraint of condition instead of the crisp sets so as to reduce the satisfaction slightly as a solution goes out of the constraint. This is a closer way to what we do in estimating alternatives in our daily lives.

It has been reported that the fuzzy linear programming contributed to the regulation of air pollution in Germany. This is a very good case. But, most of other theories have no real application yet.

In the fields of economics, marketing, and psychology, there have been some reports that fuzzy theory can be applied to many areas, including a factor analysis of customers, a structural analysis of potential consciousness, a survey of hierarchical consciousness, and an identification of human relations in a group. Alternatively, research on a fuzzy forecast and a fuzzy clustering has just started.

We have said that the idea of fuzzy theory is more appropriate to the social sciences. We expect that the advantages and the limitations of fuzzy theory will be correctly understood by many people, and fully applied to

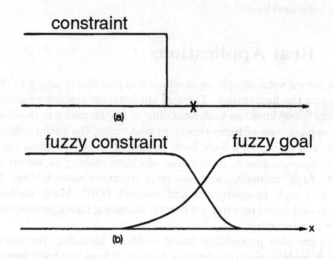

Figure 4.19: Fuzzy Decision

the social sciences and the humanities in the future.

Chapter 5

Fuzzy Computers

5.1 Demonstration of a Fuzzy Computer

We said in Section 2 that Professor Takeshi Yamakawa, Kumamoto University, presented the hardware system of a fuzzy computer at the demonstration session at the second International Fuzzy System Association Congress, Tokyo.

He demonstrated that the fuzzy computer can balance a stick (See Figure reffig-29). The fuzzy computer works the job as if a child were trying to balance a stick on his finger so that the stick won't fall when he moves his hand. We can do this game easily, but it is hard work for conventional computers.

First, we have to come up with the differential equation under an assumption that the stick is a line segment. By solving the differential equation, the computer manages to control a "truck" on which the stick is linked, which corresponding to the child's hand. To identify the differential equation, we need to know the length and the weight of the stick. Nevertheless, the demonstrated fuzzy computer made it easily without any measurement of the length or the weight.

Meanwhile, a foreign lady offered a suggestion a flower, maybe a rose or a lily. She asked to have the fuzzy computer balance the flower instead of the stick. It sounded to me almost impossible because the flower is not straight and very light. But, the fuzzy computer succeeded in making it. It surprised even Prof. Yamakawa.

He also demonstrated the robustness of the fuzzy computer. He took a computer board out of the computer and repeated the demonstration again. The fuzzy computer began to rock the stick a little, but the stick

still remained standing up.

This fuzzy computer was the first fuzzy computer in the world. The underlying theory of the computer is quite different than the well-known digital computers. What in the world is the fuzzy computer?

As we've learned, fuzzy theory deals with some uncertainty in our daily life. Since fuzzy theory was proposed, the research on fuzzy logic, which is an extension to the binary logic has been very active.

The conventional digital computer, which is based on binary logic, has some disadvantages in handling uncertain information and has no good interface with humans. As a result, we have always given way to computers. Moreover, it has been impossible for us to use the digital computer in pattern recognition or language understanding. So, what if we make a new computer based on fuzzy logic? It might be a new human-friendly computer that is capable of dealing with uncertain information. Maybe this computer will sometimes make mistakes, or output may have different answers for each time we do it. Is it really possible?

5.2 Development Work on the Fuzzy Computer

The currently developed fuzzy computer system is based on fuzzy logic. But, it is not a real fuzzy computer. It is a machine that specializes in fuzzy inferences only. The kind of all-purpose fuzzy computer that we want has not been invented yet. Fuzzy logic is a theory aiming for exact understanding of uncertainty which is allowed to be explicit. Since it is a mathematical theory, the algorithm used in the fuzzy computer must be clearly defined in the theory in order to give all steps for processing uncertain information. The goal of the programming is to allow for fuzziness but the specification of the method is not fuzzy. In this sense, what can be done in a fuzzy computer can essentially be simulated on the conventional computer in binary logic. In fact, conventional computers had been used in the experiments of the fuzzy control. The demonstration of sticks was just an experiment of fuzzy control. If the conventional computer can do whatever the fuzzy computer can do, then what is the goal of the research on fuzzy computers?

Here, let us briefly go back to fuzzy inference. We have some rules such as "if the temperature is low and the condition is the same, then put on more fuel" or "if the temperature is very high, then feed less fuel." From the rules, we can guess that when the temperature is in the middle, feed the medium amount between the two. Fuzzy inference is simulating such human inference. The uncertain expressions including more, less, very high, medium are represented in fuzzy sets. The characteristic of fuzzy inference is the idea of using fuzzy sets for representation of subjective uncertainties and the single round, rough and broad inference method. The if-then style rule is a remarkable characteristic of fuzzy inference. The degrees of conclusions are defined by the agreement degrees to the given input for each conditional part. The degrees of rules are finally aggregated to be the final output. This idea is formalized because of the introduction of fuzzy sets.

These days many applications of fuzzy logic are implemented on conventional binary logic computers. However, that way is very inefficient in terms of cost of computational power. The degree of uncertainty is represented by decimal numbers in the interval of 0 and 1, which is then fed into the numerically complex computation, though the preciseness of the decimal numbers is meaningless. Any complicated system is essentially feasible in the binary computer, but is practically impossible because of the drawback of inefficiency.

To speed up inference and reduce memory cost, instead of digital ex-

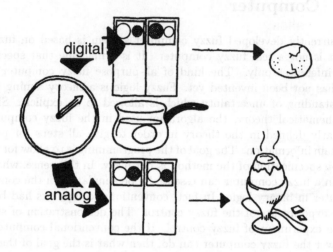

pression, the fuzzy truth value can be on analog representation in the fuzzy switching circuit and directly manipulated. The current issue in artificial intelligence and the expert systems is the treatment of the uncertainties. Fuzzy logic can provide an interesting solution to the issue. However, the solution is sometimes infeasible on the platform of the conventional computer. Efficiency is crucial, especially for the application that needs real-time processing. The demonstration system is an example of this case. We know the performance of the conventional computer which spends time in complex computation of membership values is not high enough to balance the sticks in real-time control. Therefore, we are pursuing the development of hardware for direct processing of analog values of fuzzy sets. We know that a real fuzzy computer could make more research in artificial intelligence possible. Also, under the platform of the fuzzy computer, new technologies toward truly intelligent computers could be developed. These are the reasons why the fuzzy computer is being studied.

5.3 Control Target of the Demonstration

Let us look closely at Professor Yamakawa's demonstration. In Figure 5.1, we see a moving belt attached a "truck" to which a stick is linked. The joint is not fixed and the stick is free to fall down to either the left or the right.

But, it can not be moved forward nor backward. The belt is controlled

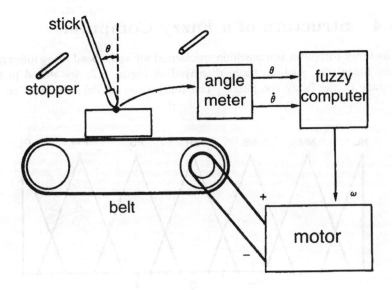

Figure 5.1: Prof. Yamakawa's Demonstration

by a motor. The angle meter is equipped at the joint and provides two values; the angle of the stick, θ, and the difference of the angle, $\dot{\theta}$. There are stoppers at both ends to restrict the movement of the stick. What the fuzzy computer has to do is to compute the rotation of the motor, ω, which addresses the horizontal location of the truck, given the angle, θ, and the difference, $\dot{\theta}$. The experiment is simplified to only one dimension from two dimensions in the actual environment. The rules used in fuzzy control are indicated in Table 5.1, where all labels are specifying fuzzy sets. The label ZR stands for Zero. The other labels, PZ, PM, PL, NS, NM, and NL are fuzzy sets to mean Positive Small, Positive Medium, Positive Large, Negative Small, Negative Medium and Negative Large, respectively. All membership functions have a simple shape. In the demonstration, only seven rules in Table 5.1 were used. Note that in this demonstration PL and NL were not used. This table shows fuzzy rules including "If θ is NM and $\dot{\theta}$ is ZR, then give ω NM," "If θ is PS and $\dot{\theta}$ is PS, then give ω PS," and so on. According to the seven rules, the fuzzy computer controls the system. The method discussed in Section 4 is similar. We can do it without solving any differential equations. Since the system is so simplified, the flower can be handled in it. As we said, any partial fault of rules can be compensated for by the other rules. The fuzzy computer is fault-tolerant.

5.4   Structure of a Fuzzy Computer

The fuzzy computer is a machine specialized for high speed fuzzy inference. Any fuzzy sets, such as those displayed in Figure 5.2, are stored in the storage of the fuzzy computer. The fuzzy rules in Table 5.1 can be set

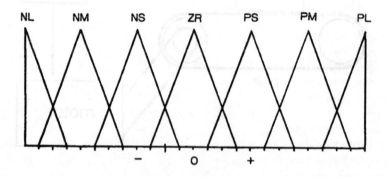

Figure 5.2: Fuzzy Sets used by the Demonstration

freely and can be modified. Fuzzy inference is executed by a series of

Table 5.1: Fuzzy Rules for Computation of ω

$\theta\backslash\theta$	NL	NM	NS	ZR	PS	PM	PL
PL							
PM							
PS			ZR		PS		
ZR		NM		ZR		PM	
NS			NS		ZR		
NM							
NL							

special IC chips which execute a single fuzzy rule for each chip. Since operations necessary in fuzzy computers are simple, such as maximum or minimum, analog circuit technologies can be used to construct a fuzzy switching function. Prof. Yamakawa's fuzzy computer has the 25 input subsets partitioned, as in Table 5.1, and 25 elements for representation of a single fuzzy set. The membership values are indicated in the voltage, ranging from 0 volt to 5 volts, meaning truth values of 0 and 1, respectively. The computational time, which is independent of the number of rules, is a constant of 10 nanoseconds. The possible inferences per second is 10 million.

There was one more fuzzy computer implementation which was supposed to be demonstrated at the second International Fuzzy System Association Congress. But, the demonstration was canceled because of U.S. export regulations. The system was developed by Dr. Togai and Dr. Watanabe, at AT&T Bell Laboratories. As in Prof. Yamakawa's approach, they developed a high speed fuzzy inference machine using a special IC for fuzzy inferences. In order to be controlled from the conventional digital computers, the IC was implemented using digital technologies. The truth value was quantified within 16 grades which were expressed in 4-bit binary signals. A membership function was defined by 16 points, thus 16 times 4 bits, totals 64 binary lines for one fuzzy set. The possible inferences per second was 250,000.

The difference between Prof. Yamakawa's and Dr. Togai's is the platform: Prof. Yamakawa decided to adopt analogue technologies in order to achieve high speed inference, while Dr. Togai thought communication with conventional computers was more important and chose the digital technologies.

5.5 Dream of a Fuzzy Computer

Machines specialized for fuzzy inference were currently called fuzzy computers. There were also fuzzy controllers that can be referred to as fuzzy computers in a sense. But, we know there is a big difference between them; the fuzzy inference machines made by Prof. Yamakawa and Dr. Togai have a hardware device, IC, for processing fuzzy inference, while the latter fuzzy controllers are implemented by software. It follows that there is a big difference of speed. Moreover, the IC can be made very small and the cost can be reduced with mass production. In a sense, the fuzzy computer could build the next generation of computers. If so, is it feasible to develop a real complete fuzzy computer?

To develop the real fuzzy computer, we have to solve the following issues:

1. Theoretical analysis of fuzzy logic

2. Development of programming language for fuzzy computers

3. Circuit level implementation of fundamental fuzzy operations

4. Identification of the architecture of fuzzy computers

The idea of general purpose fuzzy computer has not yet been fully examined, and thus the architecture is unknown. But, the special purpose fuzzy computers, which are digital computers equipped with the fuzzy inference engines, are easily designed and will soon be available.

Since the research of artificial intelligence is now looking at the issue of uncertainties, the efficiency of fuzzy computers as the platform for prototypes systems can be demonstrated. In fact, the possibilities of fuzzy computers have already been proved by the technologies achieved by Prof. Yamakawa and Dr. Togai. These will be a great tool for fuzzy controls and expert systems. Some software systems such as fuzzy programming languages and fuzzy prolog, which have been developed on conventional digital computers, are requiring to be adapted for the fuzzy computers. The results of the research on multiple valued logic could contribute to a fuzzy switching circuit and a fuzzy memory. Also, optical or bio devices may be good for fuzzy switching circuits.

Prof. Yamakawa proposed a flexible computer integrating the fuzzy systems and the multiple-valued systems. The theme of general purpose fuzzy computers is worth the challenge. There must be some relationship to the neural networks and the bio computers, which will need to be clarified step by step.

Chapter 6

Usefulness of Uncertainty

6.1   Importance of Uncertainties

We can not talk about gambling without uncertainty. The uncertainty, called randomness, is discussed in probability. It is over 300 years since probability was thought about. However, uncertainty with regards to our subjectivity has not been distinguished from randomness until recently. As seen before, uncertainty is the fuzziness for which fuzzy theory is formalized. It has been 30 years since it was theorized.

While our life is surrounded with many uncertainties, including randomness and fuzziness, all uncertainties have not been studied. Thus, please note that the theories about randomness and fuzziness are not perfect to deal with all uncertainties. A true theory of uncertainty, which is supposed to clarify properties of all uncertainties and apply the principles into broad areas, will be required in the coming century. The theory of uncertainty includes probability and fuzzy theory as a special case, though there seems to be a big gap from probability to fuzzy theory. Presumably, it took 300 years to develop the theories based on binary logic, the world of 0 and 1, only to find the limitation of it. Fuzzy theory has had a great impact on our life because it makes us notice the existence of uncertainty. We have now come into the generation when uncertainty is acknowledged as an effective and necessary concept for our life.

Human communication involves uncertainties. Imagine a communication in such words are restricted within mathematically defined ways and claims are always clear. It would be less creative communication. We can come up with a new idea from conversation with others because the semantics of language are not unique and thus can be interpreted in different ways. Even misunderstanding is useful for creative works. Because of this flexibility, we can understand each other. Uncertainty plays a key role in allowance, open-mindedness, flexibility, and interaction among human being. Uncertainty is paramount in providing incentive, acknowledgment, and allowance for others. Culture does not grow in strictly regulated and managed society. An uncertainty-free society would lose its humanity.

For instance, you are giving direction to a car driver. The direction "take right at the intersection" makes sense to the driver. That is because he is human. However, what will happen if you tell this direction to a computer? You need to specify in detail the numerical values, e.g., how much to slow down at the intersection, how much to turn the wheel, and so on. It is comfortable for us just to make a rough statement without specifying the details. This is normal human treatment. Even if the statement is not complete at the beginning, it can be fixed step by steps while the car is approaching the target. Furthermore, in the real world we often accept contradictions and counterexamples. It is an advantage of uncertainty that rough, incomplete, or inconsistent statements can be accepted as they are. We can relax when we leave the world of 0 and 1 for the sea of uncertainty, because we are human.

6.2 Use of Uncertainty

Let's look at a practical instance of uncertainty — a face chart, or a face graph. For example, the economic condition in Japan can be represented by a smiling face which means good, or a crying one which means poor.

You know what the cockpit of airplane looks like. There are enormous number of meters which displays the condition of the airplane. Presumably, it would be hard to find a problem in the airplane by just looking at the all meters. Once something happens, the pilot is required to identify the fault out of the number of meters. He would panic. Only a well trained pilot can make it. I would give up. Fortunately, we have a face chart, in which the angle of the eyebrows is linked to the hand of a particular meter. The angles of the mouth and eye also correspond to some meters. When all meters show normal condition, the face is designed to be smiling. If an eyebrow looks bad, we can find that the corresponding meter shows an abnormal value. It is a user-friendly interface. How looking at the face provides us with useful information about problems, a little like the doctor learning the condition or the disease from the face of a patient.

The two examples of the face chart, designed by Prof. Fumio Hara, are shown in Figure 6.1. The system changes not only the angle but also the

Figure 6.1: Face Chart

color. In the example of the face chart, the accurate value (the hand of meter) is made into uncertain information (translated angle of eyebrows and mouth) in order to stimulate our feelings. The uncertain information is more appropriate for getting our attention than detailed digital information. You can see the necessity of uncertain interface between humans and machines. The face chart is an example which shows that uncertain information is preferable.

Here is another familiar example of the advantages of being uncertain. You may often make the transfer from a subway line to other subway line. Using one ticket for both is a big problem. It is very expensive to examine all transfer tickets. Then, what is done with transfer? A small sample is taken and computed using a percentage of customers to estimate the true percentage of the population. Based on the percentage, several subway companies can balance their accounts. The cost for computation is very low and thus the transfer system is deployed fully. It is one merit of uncertainty.

Similar discussions can be made about regulation laws. If regulations are too precise they always fail because people find loopholes. A new regulation is drafted to close the loophole. But a new loophole will be found soon, then a new regulation has to be established, and so on. It looks like an infinite loop. The regulations become too complex. Instead, leaving some uncertainty can work for all cases. It is also useful for simplification.

6.3   Uncertainty and Organizations

Organizations are systems of humans. In early times the organization was just a set of humans. Recently, the organization is being treated as a system in systems science and engineering.

However, the system consisting of humans has some disagreements with the system of machines, though both systems may have a common target. Firstly, the system of humans has a target with a degree of satisfaction because a factor of the system is a human who has an incentive. Second, the system of humans can (and should) be adaptive to the dynamics of the environment and be an open system.

Here we face the particular issues of organizations, the lack of humanity, and the loss of flexibility, which leads to low efficiency. The organization in which all elements are scheduled and monitored reduces individual incentive. In Japan, we now face this issue, that is, the bureaucratic government.

Recently, the results of a new study on adaptive organizations in unstable environment was presented. However, in studying organizations, an important point researchers sometimes ignore is how to provide dynamics to an organization so that individual subjects are carefully protected? Here, we consider the role of uncertainty in organizations.

Suppose that an uncertainty-free organization consists of 0 and 1. What is the difference between the live organization and the uncertainty-free organization? Freedom! Freedom comes from rough connections among subsystems. Freedom also comes from the unrestricted functions of subsystems. Our incentive is generated where individual effort is allowed and encouraged. Hence, the organization can be adaptive no matter how the environment is changed because of the freedom of the subsystems. I believe that the uncertainty in Japanese organizations created by the idea that employees are generalists, not specialists, is one of the reasons why Japan's economy could grow to be stronger than other countries.

lack of humanity

low incentive

Fuzzy theory is expected to be an important tool for treatment of uncertainty, though it does not seem to cover all uncertainties. It is a good possibility that fuzzy theory can be applied to an organization, a system of humans, since it works well for a system of machines, such as expert systems, man-machine-interface, and design and operation of systems. The best strategy to activate an organization is to acknowledge uncertainty and provide flexibility.

There were many successful examples where a method established in science and technology is also available to social science. Probability and statistics are two examples. Hopefully, fuzzy theory will be applied to study organizations and contribute much to the dynamics of organizations.

6.4   Uncertainty and Politicians

The dark side of uncertainty has been emphasized for a long time, but there are many advantages as we have seen here. In our daily life, uncertainty helps to smooth communication. We sometimes talk and write in an uncertain way to show a broad meaning. Uncertain expressions can be interpreted in different ways when people receive them. While it may lead to misunderstanding, it allows for free imagination.. Uncertainty has both sides. This article itself has some ambiguous statements. Mostly, these were my fault, that is, my thoughts were not well organized, or my consideration was less careful at some points. The bad news is you can not understand my thoughts. The good news is as follows: you may have a question about that point, then think by yourself. You follow your own thoughts and interpretation, which works well for your imagination. You could achieve higher levels of understanding, which may not be intended by me. It is often the case that one can get a helpful hint from someone else who did not expect you to. You may find this is a poor excuse for giving ambiguous statements though.

A swindler cheats using ambiguity in communication. The talent for ambiguous statements is seemingly necessary for politicians, especially for Japanese politicians.

Recently, I have found many articles using the term fuzzy in newspapers, and have also found many of them pointed out a relationship to politicians. For example, the following were columns which mentioned fuzzy theory and politicians.

> "Junichirou Tanizaki, a writer, was longing for ambiguity in literature. He claimed that it is important for writing not to make everything too clear. But, his claim has been put into practice only by politicians. (Aug 25, 1985, Asahi newspaper)"

> "The second Fuzzy System Symposium, a conference for researchers pursuing ambiguity, will be held in Tokyo. The most appropriate keynote speaker is Mr. Takeshita, the chairperson of the Liberal Democratic Party, because he has been ambigu-

ous about whether or not he belongs to the Tanaka faction. (June 18, 1987, Mainichi Newspaper)"

"Fuzzy theory is interesting as a methodology in social science and may be suitable to Japanese. The ambiguities that we deal with are very broad and complicated. Thus, the successful study on various Japanese ambiguities should be awarded a Nobel prize. Today is judgment day of the appeal by ex-prime minister Tanaka. We hope it will be digital not fuzzy. (July 29, 1987 Nihon Keizai Newspaper)"

"It was developed in the U.S 20 years ago, and has been implemented in Japan. It must be something to do with oriental ideology. It reminds me that Mr. Fuzzy, Prime Minister Takeshita, is visiting Europe. We are afraid that he could not make them understand because of his ambiguity.. (June 4, 1988, Yomiuri Newpaper)"

As we can see, Japanese mass media actually likes to link fuzzy theory and politicians.

6.5   Advantages of Fuzzy Theory

Let us summarize fuzzy theory and its advantages.

First, note that fuzzy theory provides a framework that copes with uncertainty in language, that is, subjective uncertainty. This kind of uncertainty has been dealt with in fuzzy theory for the first time.

Second, fuzzy theory provides a new method of information processing. To communicate with others, human beings use language which represents our knowledge. Fuzzy theory enables us to represent our knowledge in computers.

The third point is the most important. It is that fuzzy theory provides an interface between humans and computers. It helps to reduce friction in human-computer interactions.

The conventional computer requires fully specified procedures. Moreover, it can respond with a single definite answer. Fuzzy theory, however, can recognize human-readable procedures specified by our spoken language. The fuzzy computer considers several possible answers through uncertain reasoning and outputs all of the possibilities with grades of uncertainty. If you are required to have just one answer, you can choose one of them as the basis of your subjectivity. The final decision is made by humans. If you are

not satisfied with the answer, you can retry by giving a slightly modified membership function for the language.

Fuzzy theory, therefore, is expected in medical diagnosis. As mentioned before, the final decision is chosen by the doctor from a bunch of possible answers generated by a fuzzy computer. Hence, a patient is quite free from computer fault. We definitely prefer having consultation with humans than machines. Fuzzy theory makes computers good assistants for us. We need not to bow to computers any more. The computer can be adapted to us. In terms of human-computer interaction, the most important point is to accelerate human imagination by computer-aided uncertain information processing which gives an impulse to our inspiration. Having computers work in numerical and automated processing, we can concentrate on true creative works. This relationship between humans and computers is what we would like to have in the information oriented society. Fuzzy theory is expected to implement the ideal relationship. You might see why research on uncertainties including fuzzy theory will be a buzzword in the 21st century.

Some might suggest that when computers cope with not only our knowledge but also our subjectivity, the world could exclude humans. However, the goal of fuzzy theory is the opposite of excluding humans. Fuzzy theory is working toward a human-oriented society with computers that cope with our uncertainty. Fuzzy theory disagrees with the rationalism where individual uncertainties are averaged and treated as objects. Michio Sugeno, a professor at Tokyo Institute of Technology, claims that fuzzy theory is subjective science not science of subjectivty. I personally believe that the greatest advantage of fuzzy theory is that computers can be made to be our good partners.

6.6 Frequent Questions about Fuzzy Theory

Let me close this article by answering frequently asked questions on fuzzy theory.

We know that fuzzy theory provides semantics to a computer, which is a machine that treats the semantics as symbols and thus does not understand the true meaning of the symbols. This sounds inconsistent. Which is a true statement - fuzzy theory can cope with semantics, or cannot?

In section 3, we learned that a fuzzy set is defined by a membership function, which means the semantics of the label. For example, a fuzzy set labeled with "middle-aged" (which is a symbol) has semantics represented by the membership function in Figure 3.2. In fact, the membership function is not true semantics. It approximates the semantics with fine-grained symbols. Both the label of "middle-aged" and the membership function are symbols. They differ in exactness - Figure 3.2 expresses true semantics better than the label. The relationship between a fuzzy set and a membership function is a model of semantics and symbols in our language. The membership function is appropriate for computer processing because it expresses with values. What we need to remember is how a computer treats semantics with syntax. A computer, which is a machine that has no consciousness, can not understand the true semantics of language.

The second frequently-asked question is does a fuzzy set actually have uncertainties even after a specific membership function is given? Does it deal with uncertainties?

As we have seen in Figure 3.9, answering with 0.8 is more comfortable for us than being forced to answer either 0 or 1. The value 0.8 represents our feelings which are not exactly 1 nor 0, but are closer to 1 than 0. However, it is a number defined mathematically without ambiguity. For example, 0.79 is not equal to 0.8. Then, you may try to answer by an interval from 0.6 through 0.9. However, the values 0.6 and 0.9 are certain numbers. Then, you can answer from interval to interval.... No way! That can be repeated infinitely. What I would like to stress here is that anything which allows any uncertainties can represent the original concept better than before.

No matter how you express uncertainties, the expressed uncertainty should be clear. This is the limitation of mathematical theory. Therefore, the difference between partially uncertain representation and the original concept has some uncertainty. Fuzzy theory provides clearly defined methods for approximating uncertainties. It is the first attempt toward dealing with uncertainties with respect to our subjectity.

The third question is about the paradox of whether or not the digital computers based on theory consisting of only 0 and 1 can deal with fuzzy sets.

The uncertainties represented by fuzzy sets are symbolic approximations. That is why digital technologies can not represent it with digits of 0 and 1. It should be noticed that the digital implementation is inefficient and thus a fuzzy computer is required, as we saw in Section 5.

6.7   Conclusions

In section 1, we learned that from the limitation of contemporary rationalism arose the requirement of fuzzy theory. Does fuzzy theory really exceed Descartes rationalism? Here are my personal thoughts.

It is true that the conventional approaches in science tend to discard uncertainties as much as possible. It is also true that essentially uncertain objects are out of our scope. However, as we are closely involved in systems, the requirement for our uncertainties to be recognized by computers becomes significant, and fuzzy theory can play an important role in the human-computer interaction. In this sense, fuzzy theory exceeds conventional theories, though the meta-language of fuzzy theory is defined in binary logic.

Hence, it can be considered that fuzzy theory goes along with contemporary rationalism and extends the universe of discourse. The main interest of fuzzy theory is in the methodologies used to deal with uncertainties as objects. There is a hierarchy of meta (methods) and objectives (uncertainties), which may make the previous questions arise. Fuzzy theory is a science of our subjective uncertainty. It depends on us as to how fuzzy theory will be developed. Since fuzzy theory concerns our knowledge, the impact that fuzzy theory achieves could be great for our society.

It is ridiculous that researchers who blindly trust the conventional science criticize fuzzy theory, and the researchers of fuzzy theory are offended with them. Some strange claims say fuzzy theory comes from Oriental knowledge and is better than Western knowledge. Social scientists would laugh if they heard the criticisms. From the view of social scientists, they regard fuzzy theory as one of the conventional scientific technologies.

From the discussion we have had, we observed that the development of science technologies is making enough progress to deal with human uncertainties. Social scientists who have negative impressions to fuzzy theory may have a problem - they have no theory except probability to study human behavior, though their main target is very uncertain. I think fuzzy theory is an appropriate framework for their studies.